7 Secrets of the

Sensitive

Harness the Empath's

Hidden Power

By

Diane Kathrine

Rev 3

First Printed 2016

ISBN 9781532979170

To the Empaths of

the World

With Love

Contents

Introduction

The known definition of an Empath is of a person capable of feeling the emotions of others although they, themselves, are not going through the same situation... Yet there is so much more to being an Empath.

Empaths are wired differently than most. They get overwhelmed by being around others and are overly receptive to sensory stimuli. Most have a powerful intuition, that goes way beyond instinct, and experience some amazing synchronicities. But the majority of Empaths are unaware of just where their abilities can take them in life.

Being an Empath is not easy, it is both a challenging and emotional path to walk. But, once they discover how to unleash their hidden power, it becomes an incredible and fascinating journey. This happens when they come to understand their abilities and learn the necessary steps to find balance. Within this book, I present those steps to you.

I am not too keen on labels, they dismiss individuality, but sometimes they are necessary for self-recognition. Being given the classification of an Empath helps many understand who they are and allows them to embrace their traits. This in turn helps with life navigation. That said, anyone who is Sensitive is also unique in their own right and should always bear this in mind.

~

It was back in 2011 when I started my blog, writing about ways to help the Empath discover who they are and recognize why they felt all they did. It was my intention to help them find balance and happiness, and thus become empowered. I wanted to help because I knew how difficult this road can be.

When I first started my blog, I did it out of passion and a desire to serve. Over the past years my life has seen many incredible, transformative changes. They are changes that have come about by my putting into practice all I have learnt on this path. I now know it is time to reveal more of what I have discovered, so you too can experience these amazing changes for yourself. It is my belief that once an Empath understands their abilities, and finds balance, their amazing gift will help "heal the world".

~

Before you get into The Secrets I feel it is only right that I tell you a little about myself: Like many of you, I spent the majority of my early adult years battling with powerful emotions that overwhelmed me. I used to believe these emotions held me back and stopped me from finding my "true-life-purpose". They didn't, they drew me towards it, but I had to go the long way around to make that discovery.

I grew up in what seemed like a low-income family. We were not poor but my parents were very prudent towards money. I always felt my parents were never truly happy in life. They always seeming to be stressed or angry.

My father's anger had a huge impact on me as a child. I wrongly assumed he was angry because he had money issues. I later came to realize it was because he did not feel in control of his life, and carried a lot of fear, but a seed had been planted in my brain that money was the key to happiness.

Because I grew up believing money was fundamental for a joyful life it became my intention to make some. In my mid-twenties, I went about making this happen and went into business. Taking a long-story short, I came to realize that money did not buy happiness or peace of mind. It may have bought spending freedom but not emotional freedom. (I am not suggesting living in poverty brings happiness, far from it, but when money is the driving-force of our life there will never be enough. Living happily in abundance and being driven purely by money are two different things). And so, my quest continued. I did not know it back then, but I had many more hurdles to overcome, and discoveries to make, before I was to feel the sense of contentment and emotional freedom I yearned for.

In my late twenties, I found myself drawn to the spiritual path. Although I found many answers on this road, transformations didn't start to happen until I discovered I was an Empath.

Before I knew I was an Empath, I did not understand why I had such strong feelings when around certain people or places. Some people made me sad, some filled me with negativity, some would bring out a darker-side in me, some would make me feel ill and then there were some who made me feel as though my mouth had been sewn-up. I was baffled as to why I had these all-consuming emotions, when around certain people. In time, I discovered, like all Empaths do, the majority did not belong to me. I was highly attuned to other people's energy. There were some who had the most amazing vibes and were a joy to be with but, as is human nature, I tended to focus on the more negative, of what I felt in others, and allowed it to overwhelm me.

Because I felt negativity, that I could not switch off from, in such an overwhelming way, it made me feel weak. I did not want others to know this, and use it against me, so I hid what I felt and never expressed to anyone what was going on inside my body or mind. It may have appeared to others I was being self-important, aloof or selfish, I wasn't. I had to stay disconnected to protect myself—although I didn't realize that was what I was doing—from those who made me feel bad. But this detachment was misconstrued by some and interpreted as snobbery which only made things more uncomfortable.

I felt like I was in a no-win situation. If I opened myself up to others I got drained; if I closed myself down I was attacked. Explaining my Empath ways didn't help either because people find it difficult to understand what they themselves don't experience.

It took me many years to appreciate my Sensitive nature is a rare and unique gift. When I discovered I was Empath my life made sense but it wasn't until I found balance in mind, body and spirit that I came to discover the true power of an Empath, find stability and thus self-acceptance.

Uncovering why I felt all I did, when around people, was just the start of my Empath journey. If I had not experienced all I did the path I would have followed would be unrecognizable to the one I have. The way I felt kept me searching, looking for the answers in many places. As you may have already discovered for yourself, when we keep searching, and asking the right questions, we will eventually find our answers.

To find balance and manage all that I experienced as an Empath, I have spent the past twenty years searching and studying. I studied everything from human anatomy to UFO phenomena. I am a qualified color and crystal therapist, massage therapist, reflexologist, aromatherapist, Reconnective healing practitioner, and yoga teacher. I have also spent many years doing in-depth research into diet and nutrition, and how it affects Sensitive people. My years of study and self-trials have more than paid off; restoring my health, happiness and passion for life. It is this research that also enabled me to bring to you '7 Secrets of the Sensitive'. By the time you have read this book you will understand:

- Why Empaths feel everything so powerfully.
- What their dominant and sometimes overpowering gut sensations mean.
- The overwhelming emotional overload they experience and how to overcome it.
- How Empath fatigue affects their life and who or what causes it.
- Why they attract certain types (including narcissists) and repel others.

- Why they form instant dislikes for certain people.
- Inauthentic behavior and how it weakens them.
- Trauma triggers and their causes.
- How to recognize psychic attack and how to protect from it.
- Thoughtbombing, what it is and how to stop it.
- How to tell the difference between your emotions and those which don't belong to you.
- Why parts of the Empath brain overreact to emotions and ways to prevent this from happening.
- Projection: and how you project out what you think and feel.
- The disruption of the physical and energetic glands (chakras)and how they affect the body and mind.
- How and why certain foods destroy the Empath's wellbeing.

Within this book, I help you understand why you experience what you do. I show simple steps you can take to transform your life, take back your power and live the life for which you were destined…

Secret 1

The Empath Unveiled

Who are the Empaths?

Empaths are both contradictions and enigmas, and are complex in the most mysterious of ways. Their life story is made up of many multi-faceted experiences and their unique ways set them apart. They prove to be a huge puzzlement to those who are not Sensitive and their quiet nature is often misinterpreted.

Empaths crave authenticity. This trait makes living in a world based on lies a confusing and shocking place to be. They may

1

not yet know it, but they strive to find the truth in everything and they do this by gaining knowledge. They need answers to understand the complexities of life but, most of all, they need to understand everything about themselves.

They encompass incredible emotional intelligence which they use to make careful life decisions and bring balance into their life and the lives of others. But as emotional intelligence is a rare gift, in a world ran by logic and rules, it can leave the Empath hurt and vulnerable by those who do not share this same ability.

Sensing all they do about people and life situations, makes the Empath an excellent judge of character. Their first impressions are always correct and their gut instinct is invariably spot on.

Sensing emotions so fiercely, both their own and others', often weakens the Empath. Especially if they regularly absorb emotional pain. This weakness causes conflict within their intuitive awareness of who they know themselves to be. Deep down they know they are here to do something important. But, being in constant battle with sensitivities and strong emotions, they find it almost impossible to uncover this purpose

It is too easy for an Empath to become engulfed in emotional energy, from which they will always look for ways to shelter.

The overwhelm these emotions cause often push the Empath towards vices such as alcohol, drugs or drug-like food, in a bid to numb the feelings. It may take a while to discover these vices have the opposite effect and make emotional pain more intense. In time, all Empaths come to understand only the strong could endure what they do, emotionally. This knowing, and striving for balance, eventually quells the desire to consume alcohol or other mind-altering-stimulants. With guidance and personal commitment, Empaths learn to navigate the myriad of emotional debris they face, both their own and that left by others. This allows them to take the necessary steps to create the magical and well-balanced life they desire.

Empaths often express multiple faces and personality behaviors. Depending on how they feel, who they are with or what they have picked up energetically, will depend on which face they show the world. When happy, they are an absolute joy to be around, when unhappy, or overwhelmed, they can appear morose or even arrogant. For this reason, they want nothing more than to retreat into their private sanctuaries. They need to unplug and retreat from the world in order to recharge and rebalance.

They are known as life's listeners because nothing makes an Empath happier than to listen to other people's life stories. For most of the time, the Empath prefers to listen than to share their own tales (although they can boast of several amazing life-experiences). They like to be heard but only share their problems with those who they trust. In many cases, they don't relay their own emotional woes so as not to burden or bring others down.

An Empath will often be open and welcoming to those who emit positive, warm and loving energy. They become adept at blocking out those who cause them pain, steal their joy or act in a narcissistic way.

When in balance, an Empath will recall vivid and mystically moving dreams. They can differentiate between dreams which have meaning and those which are the subconscious' way of de-cluttering the day. It is common, when they are open to it, for them to receive spiritual visitations in their dreams from loved ones.

Empaths are mostly kind, peaceful people who dislike confrontation. It is only when they are defending themselves that a nasty-side may be seen (or if they have spent too much time around negative people). If words are expressed in anger, which may hurt another, it will trouble the Empath for long after they have been said. They would rather avoid conflict, and walk away from situations that may cause it, than to hurt others.

Although forgiving, Empaths do not forget. Any emotional pain, caused by others, will leave a deep wound that can be reopened by any similar course of action. To protect themselves they often cut people out of their life who have hurt them.

Witnessing acts of cruelty, whether to human or animal, is unbearable for the Empath to endure. Seeing all the atrocities and violence in the world will stop them from watching the news or reading papers.

Most Empaths know stuff without being told. It's called the 'Knowing' and goes way beyond simple intuition. The more attuned the Empath the stronger this gift of intuition becomes. Intuition comes in many forms such as: foreseeing future events, being psychic or having the ability to read others. Not wanting to appear special or different from others, many keep this ability to themselves.

Most Empaths, especially as children, experience some type of supernatural phenomena. Sensing presences, seeing auras or knowing information others don't are just a few ways these phenomena is experienced. With age, they may switch off this gift but it never truly goes away. When, or if, the Empath is ready a teacher will appear—whether in the shape of a book, person or group—to help reactivate these innate traits.

As young children, Empaths are often open and loving, and do not understand cruel behavior even within other children. But if they suffered vicious or bullying treatment or if they were on the receiving end of many angry outbursts, the unaware Empath may find they too adopt these behavior patterns. Believing that becoming the predator, and not the prey, will protect them is a typical response of those wanting to prevent others causing them more pain. If this becomes an Empath behavior pattern it will cause them great unhappiness until they realign with their Empathic ways.

Empaths can project what they think or feel onto others without realizing. They can even project moods and thoughts that do not belong to them. Knowing whose emotions belong to whom may take time for the Empath to discern. It takes awareness for them not to jump on board with another's thoughts or emotions, and it takes even more awareness to prevent their projection.

Being a truth-seeker is an inherent trait of an Empath. Living authentically and confronting their integrity is essential for their healing and growth. On their journey, they come to understand they will not find emotional freedom without first facing their own truth. It may take some time for the Empath to face them, especially if they fear their truths will be used against them or used to cause conflict, but their truth will set them free!

Rejection, for an Empath, is not something they easily brush aside. It wounds them deeply. Rejection is one of the biggest causes of insecurities within the Empath. It is an inherent trait for them to be protective and faithful to anyone they let into their life. To be pushed away by those they trusted stirs up pain and may stop them allowing new people into their lives. The fear of a future repercussion is enough incentive to make the Empath reject others.

An Empath's mood can shift at lightening-speed. One minute they are filled with the joys of spring the next they feel low or desperately sad. These mood swings may initially cause frustration but once the root cause is understood—which is mostly being "peopled" or picking up too much emotional energy—they become better tolerated and just another aspect of Empath life.

Empaths are creative and drawn to many of the arts. The ability to imagine the unimaginable in their mind's eye allows them to create the most magical and mysterious of stories. Scripting narratives, plucked straight from their imagination, is both an elevating and cathartic pastime. Music is also uplifting in magnificent ways for Empaths. They often find the songs they are drawn to elicit powerful inner-vibrations which they easily get lost in it. Lyrics of a song may evoke strong emotions, within the Empath, leaving them awash with happy or sad tears. Freeing their voice, through song, is a liberating experience, particularly if they find verbal expression challenging.

An Empath will find the answers to anything they need to if they focus their awareness on the question they want answered. It may not be instant, but it will come in a matter of hours, days, weeks or years. The answer is not always direct, it may be given through a series of life experiences, but their Knowing will always guide them towards it. Whether they accept the answer, or not, is another story.

Multi-tasking for the Empath may prove to be a challenge as they need to focus on one thing at a time. Their awareness goes where their mind and focus is. If they are given too many tasks at once they will make mistakes or not do them efficiently. If something distracts the Empath it often throws them off the task-in-hand.

If an assignment does not stimulate or engage the Empath, they will go to a place which provides them with hours of entertainment... their mind. Empaths love to daydream and indulge their thoughts. They love to get lost within their wandering contemplations whilst the rest of the world passes them by. The downside to this trait is Empaths are prone to brain-ache from over-thinking, and if they overindulge on dark, repetitive thoughts it will leave them in a depressed state.

Empaths exude a powerful heart-brain connection. Although they are not always aware of it, they use their heart's intuitive intelligence to guide their decisions and intellect. Once honed, this ability prevents poor life-decisions and enables the Empath to help find ways to make the world a better place.

More Empath Quirks

Here are some more Empath traits which will be further broken down and scrutinized later on in the book:

Becomes Overwhelmed When in Public Places

Train stations, shopping malls, stadiums or airports, where lots of people are around, often fills the Empath with a surge of random emotions. These emotions generally don't belong to them but are coming from strangers. The overwhelm this causes may eventually lead to a phobia of public places. But the good news is there are many ways to tackle this overwhelm which will be covered later.

Certain People Cause Discomfort

When an Empath comes across inauthenticity, or people who are hiding something, it is common for their wires to get scrambled and their thought process to shut down (This can be seen as stumbling over words or the memory being affected). This is a caused by the Empathic antenna sensing something is not right.

Anyone who is not emanating truthful vibes will put an Empath on high alert, which in turn can cause emotional, physical or mental discomfort.

Senses Vibrations in Objects, Buildings or Places

History leaves an energetic imprint which an Empath picks up on. Happy, sad, angry or painful events leave potent residual energy. The more magnificent, violent or negative the event, the deeper the imprint and the more it is sensed by the Empath.

Becomes Drained After Socializing

Because an Empath feels, and takes on, the energy of others they become over-stimulated after spending time in social settings. This stimulus generally leads to fatigue and is another reason Empaths use alcohol, when socializing, either to numb the energy of others or to give them the momentum to remain sociable.

Notices Things Others Don't

Many Empaths don't realize they own this trait because they assume everyone has this ability. Empaths notice a change in people's moods, a shift in the vibration of someone's voice when they are uncomfortable; a flicker of an eye that shows another has been incensed or an inconsistency in a story. They can walk into a room and see the discrepancies others don't: a picture off center, a crack on a wall, dust on a blind or someone behaving out of character.

Reads the Energy in Others

Being able to read another is effortless for the Empath. It is like cold reading except most Empaths don't do it on purpose. When in the presence of a stranger an awareness often comes to them about who this person is. Voice vibrations and micro-movements are also revealing to the Empath; they receive this information without looking. However, when they realize they have this ability, many Empaths close it down as it can feel too intrusive.

Hypersensitive

Empaths are often told they are overly sensitive and take things too personally. Being sensitive goes hand-in-hand with being an Empath and cannot be changed.

Empaths feel everything deeply. It is something others find difficult to understand, either because they lack empathy or they've not experienced it for themselves.

Senses Emotions

Empaths sense emotions off people, both near and far. They may not be able to define the cause of the emotion, despite the fact it overwhelms them, but they experience it as their own. Although it may take a while for them to develop the skill, most Empaths eventually become adept at defining their own emotions from others' and are able to zone out from them.

Picks up Physical Symptoms

Not only will an Empath feel peoples' emotional pain, and take it on as their own, they may also develop the ailments. When out-of-balance, or rundown, the Empath may experience irritations, ailments and body aches like sympathy pains that belong to those they frequently come into contact with. They may even briefly take on the physical pain, or symptoms, of a stranger who they happen to be in the proximity of.

Abhors Narcissism

There is often a love/hate relationship between the Empath and the narcissist. Most will have had a bad experience with one at some point in their lives. Where you find an Empath, you will often find a narcissist close by. Although kind and tolerant of others, Empaths dislike to be around overly egotistical people.

Those who put themselves first and refuse to consider anyone's feelings, or points of view, other than their own—like the narcissist so often does—deflates an Empath.

Has Heightened Senses

All humans are sensory beings, meaning we regulate certain data through the given senses: sight, sound, taste, touch and smell. In those who are Sensitive these senses are heightened: sounds may be louder, sights more vivid and harder to define and aromas more potent.

Gets Upset by People's Insensitivity

Because Empaths are considerate and have incredible empathy, often putting the needs of others first, they get upset when others do not show the same consideration. If someone they care about lets them down it wounds the Empath deeply. Because they have such strong empathy it is hard for them to rationalize with those who don't.

Welcome to the Wonderful World of Empaths

If you, or someone you love, is an Empath life will never be dull. But it may be challenging. The Sensitive are here, at this time, for a reason and it is not by chance they were born with such awareness and heightened senses. Sadly, because they have spent much of their life becoming overwhelmed by all they feel and pick up, they may not have been able to fulfil these destined roles. And this is what I hope to change within the pages of this book.

The modern world may seem more like hell for an Empath, rather than the place where dreams come into fruition. The reason their world appears to be so hellish is often because they are out-of-balance within their mind, body or spirit. Everything from the food they eat to the energy people emit can have a detrimental effect and contribute to a lack of stability, stamina and enthusiasm. Some Empaths are now so out-of-balance that they do not know where to start in healing their lives. But once they uncover the roots of their physical and emotional discomforts, and the steps towards realignment, the unhappy, unbalanced Empath becomes a thing of the past and the empowered Empath steps forward.

We all experience hardships at some point in our lifetime. Life difficulties are all part of a bigger picture and serve in many amazing ways. It is in the tough times we learn the most. By facing hardships growth happens and you move forwards towards a greater place. However, you do not need to keep experiencing the same old emotional pain and un-pleasantries for a lifetime - like many Empaths do.

Unveiling the secrets of their ways is just the start of an incredible journey of growth for the Empath. When they find balance, and uncover their hidden power, the Empath's vibration elevates phenomenally and their true magnificence is revealed to them. But, if you want to see this positive transformation, you have to put in the work and make the necessary changes.

Change takes commitment and dedication and you are the only one who can make it happen. If you want to see change, you have to make change!

When you listen, your inner-guidance will guide you towards the necessary steps to take for life transformation. This book was one of those nudges from your higher self. You were guided towards it because you are ready. It wasn't coincidence that you came across it, it was destiny's way of helping you find balance, uncover your hidden power and walk towards your true purpose.

Secret 2

The Gift…?

Empaths have the gift to feel. They feel the days of the week, other people's emotions, the vibration of objects and the energy of places. To "feel" is what Empaths do and is their most powerful and important gift. They feel deep empathy, experience powerful intuitive feelings, and understand others by the way they feel. Their ability to gauge the world, by the way it feels, helps the Empath navigate their way through life. It also helps protect them from making bad choices and decisions.

To some, feeling everything so powerfully may, understandably, seem more like a curse than a blessing. And until the Empath learns to control it, this gift will indeed seem to be a curse.

This gift, that could be classed as a sixth-sense, is a sense that isn't recognized by most. Claiming to have the ability to feel, and read, other people's energy may be scoffed at by those who don't themselves experience this trait, there is little an Empath can do about that. But there is no denying that Empaths get flooded by sensory stimuli, coming from the thoughts, emotions and physical state, of those they come into contact with.

The Empath's ability to "feel" could be likened to the psychic gift of clairsentience—known as the ability to sense subtle energy in inanimate objects—but the Empath also has the ability to sense, and read, energy in people and places.

All humans are sensory beings but it is known the Empath's, or highly sensitive person's, senses are heightened. They receive sensory stimuli, like everyone else, but process much more information from it than the average person. Because they don't take it on purpose, the excess energy they accumulate often becomes overwhelming. Spending time in a busy, peopled, room is often draining for the Empath, as they acquire many different energetic vibrations. Each person has their own unique frequency at which they vibrate. How individuals think and feel affects the pulse rate of these frequencies and also how they feel to an Empath. The healthier, happier and more positive the person the faster and purer their vibration is. When someone is of ill-health, angry, bitter or resentful, the slower their vibrational frequency and the worse their energy will feel to an Empath.

The Empath's ability to experience other peoples' emotions, and energy, is very real phenomena. They are simply sensing an individual's vibratory frequencies. But because it is not always recognized or understood, by those who don't have the same ability, it is difficult for them to understand. That is not to say the non-Empaths of the world don't feel other people's emotions, they do just in a subtler way. Every person senses bad moods, hostile atmospheres and other mood-related-energy impressions, but they do not feel it a fraction as powerfully as an Empath.

The Power of the Empath

Because of what they feel, or pick up emotionally from others, some Empaths go through life feeling vulnerable and cowardly.

Even if they tried to convince themselves of their true power their Sensitive nature, or not being able to switch off from external negativity, often persuades them otherwise. What I want to let you know, before we go any further, is that if you are an Empath you are stronger than you could ever imagine. There are few who could go through life feeling all you do and still get up to face another day.

The barrage of emotions an Empath endures may make them appear fragile and defenceless but that could not be further from the truth. Because they don't always understand how to control them, their emotions become the Empath's Achilles heel, which leads to a sense of vulnerability. If the techniques they use, for protection or to prevent overwhelm, do not work it may cause another sense of failure. This then instils their conviction of being defenceless.

Empaths become overstimulated by people's energy and emotions. This overstimulation has nothing to do with being weak, or a failure, it amounts to being exposed to too much stimuli for their Sensitive nature.

It is sad that so many Empaths become reclusive for the reason it is too painful, or overwhelming, to be out in public. That said, stepping away from the world often proves to be an incredible time for growth and self-reflection for the Empath. But if you find you are hiding because you cannot handle the way the world makes you feel, I hope, by the time you have finished reading this book, you will know exactly what to do to harness your inner-power and get back out there (if that is what you want).

Know Your Own

The first thing any Empath should learn to recognize, on their quest to harness their hidden power, is what emotion belongs to whom. Part of an Empath's journey is about differentiating between their emotions and those belonging to others. Knowing this helps you deal with other people's stuff. It also allows you to understand your own feelings and how to act on them accordingly. Staying aware, when in public, helps you make this ascertainment. It is too easy to take on another person's pain and mistake it as your own. Once you learn to recognize them, being able to differentiate the energies and emotions, coming from your external environment, makes life less complicated and uncomfortable.

Depending on what you are experiencing in life should depend on how you feel. If you have been in a troubled place it will affect your emotions and thoughts. If your life has been steady, with no particular ups and downs, and you are experiencing a torrent of negativity you are likely processing another person's energy. Falsely identifying with emotional energy is easy to do. You can get so wrapped up within other people's erratic energies that you do not question their origin.

So how can you tell when an emotion does not belong to you? The easiest and quickest way to make this determination is to speak to the emotions directly: When you initially sense any type of overpowering emotional energy say to yourself: if these emotions are not mine, leave me now!

If the emotions do not belong to you, and are coming from another, they promptly start to lose their grip. You will feel a definite shift in the way the emotion feels. It may be subtle but you will feel a change. When you notice this subsidence, distract yourself, immediately. Why? Because negative emotions are powerful and although they may have receded slightly they can return swiftly and with a vengeance, especially if you allow your focus to return to them. Unpleasant emotions engage unpleasant repetitive thoughts and once your thoughts get wrapped up in the emotions, belonging to others, there is no getting away from them.

Distraction is an incredible tool for keeping your mind away from unpleasant emotions—others' or indeed your own—and often works instantly.

The practise of distraction is used all the time by the governments, and people in power, to keep your attention off a subject they do not want you to focus on. Distraction is used because it works. By taking your focus off one thing and moving it to another you are effectively tricking yourselves away from an issue that was garnering your attention

Here are a handful ways to distract the mind:

- Sing a song, out loud or in your head, or listen to loud uplifting music.
- Get creative: do something engaging that you have a passion for.
- Recite poetry or a limerick.
- Get a crossword out and attempt to complete it.
- Focus on your breathing and count back each breath from three hundred or practice pranayama.
- Give yourself a complex equation to figure out or go through the alphabet backwards.

- Do some vigorous exercise, dance or do a full body shake.

Psychic Attack

Sometimes, when you suddenly feel overbearing emotions you could be on the receiving end of something sinister. When entering a public place, it is easy to recognize emotions as belonging to others. It is more difficult, however, to discern emotional energy when alone. It is common for the Empath to sense negative emotions, or uncomfortable energy, coming from others when there is no one around. But if you feel weird spiteful energy, when alone, you could be under some kind of psychic attack.

Psychic attack generally happens when another is having bad thoughts about you. More often than not it will be a friend or family member having a bad day and using you as their mental punch-bag. Determining the origin of strange, ireful emotions takes investigation. But, if you suspect you are on the receiving end of psychic attack, you need to take a different approach than when you are simply picking up on other people's emotions.

Firstly, you need to determine who the attack is coming from. Generally, when you ask the question: 'To whom does this energy belong?' you will get a mental picture of who is sending you bad energy or having undesirable thoughts about you. The moment you know who the culprit send them love, lots and lots of love. When you bombard someone with love energy it negates all ill intentions and dark thoughts.

There is nothing more powerful than love. It is the most prevailing force there is. It may seem difficult to conjure up the feelings of love, when you have been flooded with negativity from another, but if you keep repeating: 'I send you love, I send you love,' you will eventually feel it. Love essentially neutralizes hate, resentment or bitterness (which is often the objective of psychic attack).

The Fear Belonging to Others

On your journey as an Empath it is important to recognize if a fear belongs to you or to another. Just like picking up emotions, the Empath can pick up other people's irrational fears and take them on as their own. Feeling fear is not always a bad thing, it is often a protecting force, but if it belongs to another it may unnecessarily hold you back in life.

Fear is a controlling emotion. Because it is so potent, it is the emotion Empaths frequently acquire. Fear belonging to another, feels much the same as your own and can be difficult to differentiate between. You can use the same questioning technique, as above, to discover if the fear, you feel, belongs to you or another. If in doubt to whom the fear belongs make the following statement: If this fear is not mine leave me now! Say it out loud or in your head. If it is not your fear it will start to shift.

Another quick way to discern between your fear and another's is to check if you had it prior to being in their company. For example: You may be going on holiday with a friend who has a secret fear of flying. You are super excited about the trip, that is until you sit next to your friend on the plane. She hates flying and is terrified but is trying hard not show it. When seated, you suddenly experience a wave of panic wash over you. You don't question if it's anyone else's fear because it seems so real. And, because your friend has not expressed to you, her fear of flying, you don't suspect it is coming from her You now think of nothing else but this prevailing wave of fear that is stirring up floods of panic within. It wipes away the joy and excitement, you previously felt, as you become traumatized by the panic. You then may convince yourself you are scared of flying.

But the end of the flight is not the end of the trauma. As a form of protection, your brain stores this fear, of being on the plane, ready for quick recall when you are in the same position again. It is the brain's protective way to alert you to a dangerous situation. The next time you get on a plane the brain may trigger the memory of your last flight, and the fear you felt (which belonged to your friend). This could then lead to an irrational and unnecessary fear of flying.

You do not have to be connected to a person to feel, and take on, their fear. All it takes is for you to be in their energy field. A phobia, caused by another person's fear, will wrongly hold you back in life. If you didn't have fear about a situation, or event, before being in the company of another, you have to consider that the fear may not belong to you.

Fear creates negative emotions: Negative emotions create lasting memories. If someone, or something caused, an intense fear every time you are with them, or in a similar situation, the memory of the emotion will be reignited. This is why it is important to distinguish whose fear you are in. If you are often filled with dread, or irrational fear, with no present reason, it may be caused by a ripple from your past. Excessive emotional distress causes havoc with all systems of the Empath's body, especially the brain. When it comes to processing emotional pain, your own or that which is ignited from other people's energy, the Empath's brain is unique. This subject is covered in greater detail in Secret 7. The information presented will help you understand why, as an Empath, you experience such potent emotional reactions to life situations. But for now, let's take a look at how the law of attraction impacts the Empath

The Law of Attraction...Like Attracts Like!

So, what is it and how does the law of attraction affect the Empath? Basically, if you are in a low-mood you will attract more of this type of energy towards you. If you are feeling happy, grateful and positive you will attract situations to make you feel more of this energy. Simple!

Because you receive back the same vibratory frequency as you emit it is important to keep your emotional energy as clean as possible. All low-level moods will be energetically returned. And this includes the emotions picked up from others. Because Empaths are hardwired into taking on unpleasant emotions, from those they spend time with, they often have to work harder to stay in alignment. But other people are not the only thing that unnecessarily lowers an Empath's vibration...

'We don't attract what we want, we attract what we are.'
Wayne Dyer

The way you feel is affected by many factors such as your environment, stress, diet and lifestyle choices. These aspects all affect the way your hormones (chemical messengers) and brains work.

When their hormones are out-of-balance, it wreaks havoc on the Empath's emotions and the way they perceive the emotions belonging to others. And until the chemical messengers, of your brain and body, are back in balance your emotional wellbeing will be compromised. The problem is most are unaware their hormones are out of whack or how it impacts their Empath health and happiness. If your hormones are out and negatively affect your moods, your vibration will be lower than it should be. This basically means you attract more low vibrational energy just because your hormones are influencing how you feel.

As already mentioned, everything is energy vibrating at different frequencies. People, cars, houses, trees, the birds and the bees, all possess their own unique energy signature. The more in balance an Empath is the higher their frequency and the more positive energy they attract. The problem is if your chemical messengers are disrupted, by exposing yourself to low-level people, food, environments, etc. it lowers your vibration. This in turn means you attract back more low-level energy. It becomes a vicious cycle but it is also a cycle that can be broken. This subject is covered in greater detail in Secret 6? But for now, let's take a look at how other people's thoughts can affect your Empath life.

Thoughtbombing

One thing Empaths do too much of is thinking. Overthinking can become a habit that needs addressing and got under control. But as we are talking about Empaths here, controlling thoughts is not always that straight forward. For one thing, many Empaths are unaware of just how well connected they are to other people's thoughts which they often misinterpret as their own.

I use the term "thoughtbombing" as a way to explain the ability to dive into another person's thoughts. I'm sure you have heard of photobombing, well, thoughtbombing is the same concept but instead of diving in someone else's photo you are plunging into their thoughts. The trouble with thoughtbombing is you are mostly oblivious as to when you are doing it.

It took me a long while to realize I was thoughtbombing. I didn't think it was even possible. But, if there's one thing this life has taught me: anything is possible... especially with the power of thought!

You may not be able to see or touch your thoughts but you know they are there. Thoughts are energy that vibrate at their own speed. The thoughts you indulge will create your reality and determine how you interpret the world. Because everyone is connected by a Universal Mind, or Cosmic Consciousness, it should come as no surprise that you are able to tap into other people's thoughts (consciousness) and mistake them for your own.

Empaths are open and receptive to other people's energy, fact! This can be seen in the way they pick up other people's "emotional stuff" and take it on as their own. The same thing happens with thoughts. Where emotions are generally felt around the solar-plexus, or heart area, thoughts are picked up in the mind. Any Empath can unintentionally pick up others' thoughts, but if their crown, or third eye chakras are too open then are susceptible to over-harvesting people's thoughts. (More on the chakras later).

Benign thoughts do no damage, but when they are dark, marauding or angry they can potentially cause disruption to the Empath. For example: when you pick up thoughts, in the shape of strong opinions, you may find these opinions shape your life and become the voice within your head: political opinions, strong likes or dislikes to name a few.

Thoughtbombing is easiest to recognize when with those you are connected to but it also happens when positioned nearby to someone with whom you are not acquainted. Imagine being stood in a queue when you suddenly start visualizing eating a lamb-casserole for dinner. This may not seem unusual to some but if you stopped eating lamb years ago, and have never been keen on casseroles, this idea may seem a tad random. This is a classic case of thoughtbombing, picking up another person's plans for dinner and taking them on as your own.

Ways to Recognize Thoughtbombing

- Mentioning to a friend or loved one your thoughts and they tell you they were thinking the exact same thing.
- Finding yourself having negative thoughts about someone with whom you have no qualms. This happens

after spending time with one who has an unresolved issue with said person.

- Suddenly liking something you didn't or wanting to visit a place you previously had no interest in.
- Having the urge to do something out of character.

Thoughts create reality and shape your life, they can make you happy, angry or sad. Thoughts are part of your belief system and behind your decisions. They may lead you into trouble or out of danger. In life, your thoughts hold the reins and the last thing you would want is to allow another person's thoughts, or opinions, to unknowingly shape your reality.

Some Empaths may find they thoughtbomb more than others (Even as Empaths we are all still different). It is helps to know if you are an unconscious thoughtbomber, or not, so that you can take back control.

Everyone has an average of 48 thoughts per minute or 50,000 to 70,000 thoughts a day. That's a lot of thinking. Negative thoughts often take precedence in the mind. This is because humans are hardwired into having more negative thoughts than positive. It's a condition called negativity bias and stems back to survival instincts from caveman days. Empaths often brood for hours on dark menacing thoughts whilst positive ones can be fleeting and go unnoticed. And yes, this also happens with negative thoughts that don't belong to you. You have a 17 second window in which to engage or deny a thought. Thinking bad thoughts now and then isn't a bad thing; it certainly keeps life interesting, but the problems happen when you get caught up in the negative thought process. Overindulging negative thoughts will shape your life into something you may not want (by the law of attraction). This is made worse if the thoughts were triggered by someone else's views or ideas.

Another problem with negative thinking is that your body is always listening to your thoughts. It reacts to everything you think. Negative thoughts turn into powerful emotions. Strong emotions adversely impact the endocrine glands, which then compromises the immune system. Thoughts also trigger responses within the limbic system in the brain. This can have a disagreeable bearing on your emotional life (more on that later). Allowing the body to be harmed by negative, repetitive thoughts is unnecessary and, if the negativity has come from another person, it is preventable. Being vigilante of when you are thoughtbombing is important. Stopping yourself from doing it is essential.

So, how do you prevent thoughtbombing? Before we get to that I'll explain how projection works.

Projection

You are now aware, as an Empath, that you pick up emotions, pain and thoughts from others. But you may not be aware of how you can project what you feel out into the world. Most, who know of their ability to project, will endeavour to avoid sending out negative energy, in the way of thoughts or anger, because they understand that not only will others be on the receiving end of it, but what goes out also comes back. When you project your mood, in a peopled place, it becomes evident when others mirror your actions or dispositions. It is like emotional contagion and is similar to yawning: If you see one person yawning you often develop an irresistible urge to yawn. With projection of your own energy, however, the energy exchange is not seen. The way it is recognized is when you notice others mimicking your movements, behaviors or moods.

No matter how in control of your Empathic abilities you are, there will always be times when you switch off your awareness. When this happens, you may unintentionally project untamed energy out. What goes out comes back. If you send negative thoughts out, you pick them back up with interest. Unfortunately, all Empaths have to stay aware and vigilante of what they project. To prevent thoughtbombing you also have to be wary of projection because the two seem to go hand-in-hand. Those who unconsciously project are often the ones who unintentionally thoughtbomb.

Thoughtbombing from a Distance

I have already discussed how Empaths pick up on thoughts when near strangers. You do not have to be, in any way, "connected" to them to pick up their thoughts. However, thoughtbombing from a distance generally only happens with those to whom you are acquainted.

Thoughtbombing from afar is often triggered by an unspoken issue between the Empath and another. This unresolved concern may open up a "dark-thought-dialogue connection". This mostly happens when the other, involved in the dispute, deliberates about the Empath in a disapproving or nasty way (similar to psychic attack). As an Empath, you pick up on powerful thoughts even from a distance. Getting caught up in these thoughts, by lingering on them for longer than 17 seconds, will cause an energetic conflict. If you focus on their dark musings, irrational anger may well up within you. This anger is then unintentionally projected back to the person involved. They then become further incensed and their thoughts turn darker. Before you know it, you are both having a full-on negative thoughtbombing war!

It is too easy for the Empath to become embroiled in the destructive thought-loop of another. With a thought-loop, the same thought repeats over and over. If you are intertwined within someone else's dark thoughts it can make breaking the cycle difficult.

The best way to prevent—or disconnect from—the thoughtbombing process is by firstly identifying the thought's origin. The easiest way to do this, to break the psychic connection, is by questioning your thoughts:

Questioning Thoughts

- **Did this thought pop up out of nowhere?** A negative or random thought, that does not belong to you, will often come into your awareness out of the blue.

- **Does it seem like your way of thinking?** If your thoughts are angry or negative, and you rarely think that way, they probably aren't yours.

- **Is it a long-since forgotten issue?** If the thought is relating to someone or something from your long-forgotten past, it could mean the other person involved is festering on it.

- **Is the thought relating to a family member or friend of whom you would not be thinking?** When a person keeps coming into your awareness, in a negative way, of whom you've not had any recent dealings with, they may be having bad thoughts about you.

- **Does your mood quickly change?** This is a classic thoughtbombing experience: Suddenly being taken down, by a random thought that steals into your awareness, is often due to another having unpleasant thoughts, about you, and is similar to psychic attack.

It is not your job to get others to see things from your perspective and you cannot stop them from indulging in nasty thoughts about you. But, as an Empath, you can access mental spaces they can't and become embroiled in thoughts you shouldn't. It is imperative to recognize when you are thoughtbombing to stop it and block it.

Once you recognize a thought does not belong to you disengage from it and, in your mind, see it recede back. If you do not send it back it will sit in your energy field where, if you're not mindful, you can access it again. An Empath needs to stay in a high vibrational space if they want to remain in balance. This is difficult to do if they are dipping into other people's negative thought patterns.

'Your worst enemy cannot harm you as much as your own unguarded thoughts'

- Buddha

Learning to stop negative thoughts within seventeen seconds is important for all Empaths; whether they belong to you or not. Your thoughts turn into emotions and your emotions turn into stress. Stress will switch on your sympathetic nervous system SNS (fight-or-flight) which causes all kinds of imbalances and Empath fatigue. When the Empath is out-of-balance, their thoughts become erratic. This is something that can be addressed and avoided.

41

Once you have finished reading this book you will have all the tools you need to transform your life and find balance. Controlling negative thought patterns and unconscious thoughtbombing then no longer need be a problem. Healthy thoughts follow a healthy body and mind.

Although it is easy to understand why it is not seen that way, Empaths have a gift. Once you are knowledgeable of how this gift is compromised you get back in control. Gaining a greater understanding of how people affect you takes you a step further in that direction...

Secret 3

The People Factor

Spending too much time around people often causes distress for the Empath. The more disagreeable the person the more of an impact they have. That said, it does not have to be the more disagreeable people who bring the Empath down, anyone can even your nearest and dearest.

The longer an Empath has known someone the greater effect they have on their emotional energy. As you would imagine, this could be good or bad, depending on the relationship. Understanding how people affect you and knowing how to navigate your relationships will serve in offering you a healthier and happier life.

When it comes to friends, you may have noticed certain acquaintances act differently depending on whose company they are in. For example: you may have good two very good friends who when you spend time on a one-to-one basis you have a great time with. Yet put those two friends together, on a social occasion, and their energy dynamic shifts. Their collective energy may alter to such a degree that you feel drained, angered or even bullied in their presence. You may find this hard to understand because it never happens when you are alone with them. Everyone will, at some point, change their personality to adapt to the people they are with (Empaths often morph unintentionally). This change won't affect or upset most people but it may have a negative impact on the Empath. Fake or inauthentic energy is especially debilitating to the Empath, even when it is seen in good friends, and can trigger a host of uncomfortable feelings. We will look at the effects of inauthenticity shortly but, if you can relate to this, it may be advisable to see certain friends on a one-to-one basis only.

Friends' energy and how it influences those of a Sensitive nature will change along with their age and life circumstances. If down or depressed, a friend can unintentionally take the Empath down with them. In these cases, one has to learn to unplug from their energy. You can listen and still be there for them, but in a detached way. You also have to be wary of how much time you spend with them. It may seem cruel to cut short time spent with a friend in need, but staying too long in the presence of anyone filled with gloom will bring you down.

When in a certain friend's company, who is in emotional crisis, you often find yourself getting drained of energy. Every Empath has heard of those who deplete energy: otherwise known as "Energy Vampires". When a friend is experiencing a rough time in life, they may themselves, inadvertently, become the vampire.

To avoid being a friend's "energy-replacement-meal", watch for any drain and where it is coming from. It will normally be in one of the four main energy centers (chakras): The sacral chakra which is a couple of inches below the belly button, the solar-plexus chakra which is mid-belly area, the heart chakra situated over the mid-chest, or the throat chakra positioned at the front of the throat. The energy depletion can be felt as a pull or ache in the place affected. Wherever you feel it, cover the area immediately with your hands or arms. It is not by chance people cross their arms over their stomach, or chest, in social situations.

They are, subconsciously, protecting themselves from an unwanted energy drain.

Empaths are faithful to their friends and keep them in their life for the long-haul. But people change. Some develop undesirable or narcissistic traits as they age. It is healthy to release those, from your life, who bring you down or act in narcissistic way towards you. And you should not feel guilt for doing so. Friends who repeatedly bring you down become toxic to you.

Toxic friends will deplete your energy even after a short time spent in their presence. And when you pick up their toxic energy, you end up vibrating on this same frequency for a period of time. As the law of attraction dictates, you then attract more of this type energy. This helps no one.

People do not have to be emotionally down or toxic to impact the Empath. Simply spending a lot of time around others can be debilitating. Most social gatherings eventually become a chore, or a dreaded encounter, for the Empath. This is because they become overstimulated when in busy environments. This overstimulation is one of the triggers for Empath fatigue.

Empath Fatigue (E.F.)

Empath fatigue is a most challenging trait which takes the Empath out of action faster than anything. It is a mix of chronic fatigue coupled with low-moods or depression. Every Empath experiences it at some point and it is both acute and incapacitating.

Empath fatigue has several root causes. Sensitivities to the environment and diet both play a part. But a major trigger is too much social stimulation. Taking on too much energy from others can ignite a bout of E.F. that can last for days.

Fatigue is a difficult trait for an Empath to endure and is often relentless in its nature. Not only will it cause intense lethargy but it also makes the body feel like a lead weight. Merely moving a limb becomes hard work and any kind of work, or exercise, is a mammoth task.

Like a "people hangover", most experience Empath fatigue after spending time around negative or draining people. But, as already mentioned, this crushing fatigue is also activated by remaining too long in busy peopled places. It is basically being exposed to too many people for too long. Although E.F. may affect every Empath differently, it is a real side-effect of being "peopled".

So why is Empath fatigue caused by people? It is more a case of giving and receiving too much energy. I liken E.F. to food intolerances. It ignites in a similar way. With food intolerances, health problems occur after eating certain foods. An intolerance is different to a food allergy; where one can have a life-threatening reaction within minutes of ingesting an offending food. With food intolerances, one may consume small amounts of a certain food and experience no reaction. For example: If one has an intolerance to almonds, one may eat five almonds and have no reaction. However, eat eight almonds and the immune system is activated and a negative-bodily reaction occurs.

This is how Empath fatigue works, but instead of ingesting too much of an aggravating food, the Empath digests too much incompatible energy into their own energy field. This causes a reaction similar to an allergy and also activates the amygdala (part of the brain that controls the sympathetic nervous system: See Secret 7). When the amygdala is overly stimulated, it can disrupt the natural flow of hormones and contributes to a crashing burn-out.

The best way to prevent Empath fatigue is to learn your personal triggers, avoid them, and put a limit on time spent socializing.

How to Gauge Social Time-Limits

When in social situations note how you feel after. Know how long you were in the environment and how you felt later that day or the next. When in shopping malls, with friends, at parties, or other, take note. If you spend three hours with friends and feel fine the next day, you know this is a safe socializing time-limit. If spending five hours in the same company zaps you and triggers negative reactions, then this is too much time.

Every Empath has a people time-limit. For some it may be two hours for others it could be five. My time-limit is between two and four hours depending on the situation and the people. You will also have different time limits with different people.

Too much social stimuli can bring the Empath down for days, whether being at a party or spending an evening with close friends. Socializing contributes to E.F. If you want to stay in a healthy space, and avoid fatigue, you have to know your time-limits and try to stick with them.

Everyone is different, as is their social time-limits. Depending on how balanced you are, these limits will chop and change over the years. You will find the more time you spend alone the cleaner your energy becomes. The cleaner your energy the more you will react to social stimuli, and the less time you will handle in public.

When your energy-field is clear it only takes a small amount of negative energy to bring you down. The more time spent around others the more resilient you are to their energy. This does not mean it is not affecting you, you just don't react to it as quickly as when you are clean.

The Guilt Trip

It is important to avoid feeling guilt for cutting time short with friends, family or other. Guilt is an emotion many Empaths suffer with, yet serves no other purpose than making you feel bad. Empaths have to prioritize their wellbeing. Friends can make you feel guilty for leaving a party early, or not spending as much time with them as they would like, and because of this, you may stay longer than is healthy in a social situation.

If your friends know and understand of your social time-limits, you can leave an event guilt-free. If they don't, be prepared. The best way to avoid the "leaving-early-guilt-trip" is by having a valid reason to go before you even arrive. You should plan your exit strategy before you go anywhere socially. Even if it is the reason of getting up early the following morning for work, to do a chore or to hit the gym. Have it prearranged. This gives you a genuine reason for an early departure. When friends do not experience the fatigue, Empaths suffer with, after spending too much time around others, they don't understand how awful and debilitating it is. Some of the people I've known, over the years, have considered me to be a hypochondriac because of the crushing E.F. I experienced. That said, I too thought I was slightly neurotic, before I discovered I was an Empath.

When it comes to social time, Empaths need to put their own needs before other people's disappointments. This is not just for your health but for the wellbeing of others too. Once you suffer from a bout of Empath fatigue your whole energy signature changes. When emotionally or physically low there is a tendency for the Empath to project this energy out which will then impact those on the receiving end.

Preventing E.F.

Knowing your triggers is essential for preventing Empath fatigue. You may find, if you have suffered with E.F. for many years, that you get triggered by more than just people. It took me a while to discover my triggers: negative people, certain foods, long working hours, over-exercising, stress and spending too much time with friends or in busy places, but in making that discovery it was a critical component for my Empath welfare. And I have suitably adapted my lifestyle to reduce any unnecessary occurrences.

If you want to avoid the "people-hangover", it is important to know your time-limits when in peopled places or social situations. To discover this, it is a good idea to keep a fatigue/emotion diary. In it make a note of where you went, who you were with and how you felt. How did you feel for the following days? It is also advisable to write down what food and drinks you consumed as they too can contribute to E.F. It won't take long before you see a pattern and get to know your triggers and social time-limits.

Why Empaths Have Instant Dislikes for People

Everyone has instant dislikes for someone or something in their life. But in the Empath's case, these dislikes are often their intuition at work.

When an Empath has an instant dislike, for anything, it is a good indication that it should not be part of their life. You may dislike a person on first introductions, and have no particular reason for it, or you may get an instant repulsion towards another without having spoken to them. Whatever the dislike there will always be an energetic or intuitive motivation behind it.

My own natural aversions, towards certain people, have always proved to be for a reason. Although it took a while to accept this. I used to feel guilt for disliking someone I had not even talked to. It seemed like I was judging them and I did not understand why. Recently, at an event I was attending, I felt an instant dislike for a red-haired lady sitting nearby. She had no negative or dark energy around her and I knew she was not a bad person but, still, I felt this loathing towards her. As the day went on a friend, I was with, started a conversation with her when I went to the bathroom. On my return, I found the red-haired lady had moved next to my seat and was chatting to my friend. When I sat down the lady included me in the stories she was happily regaling. Within five minutes of listening to her narratives I could feel the energy being drained from me and I knew if I did not get away my energy would be zapped completely. I made my excuses and moved away.

My natural aversion to this lady was not born from my ego, making me better than her, nor was I was judging her for being a bad person. She wasn't. My intuition was warning me she was an unaware "energy drainer". If I had allowed her to drain my energy I would have been vulnerable to all the other people at the event. By giving me an instant dislike, of this lady, my inner "Knowing" was protecting me.

It is important to point out you should not feel regret for experiencing instant dislikes of others. Nor should you force yourselves to change the way you feel. Trust your intuition. Sensitive people often feel remorse for having bad feelings about another person. Especially those they do not know. But these natural aversions are there for a good reason... for protection. Think about the first time you drank alcohol, or tried smoking, you probably disliked it. This was your body telling you they were not good. You may have ignored those signals, because you wanted to drink or smoke for your own reasons, but they happened as an intuitive warning. As a child, you may have disliked milk but were told to drink it because it was good for you. When you grew up you discovered you were lactose intolerant. Your body gave you a natural dislike to stop you drinking the milk because it was harmful.

Likes and dislikes aren't always personal or lifestyle choices. Sometimes they are safety prompts born from your intuition as protection.

The Dislike of the Empath

It is not just the Empaths who take an instant dislike of others, they themselves often experience it the other way around. Everyone experiences being around someone who has taken an instant dislike to them. Empaths included. Taking a dislike to another is an acceptable part of life. Everyone is different. There will always be people with whom you do not get along. But what can endlessly puzzle the Empath, is why people act in a cold or mean-spirited way towards them when they know they are likeable and trustworthy. It makes no sense. And they are not always given a reason, when someone changes towards them, becoming stony and uncaring almost overnight.

When bizarre resentments suddenly appear, in those you have known for some time, it can cause a deep sense of hurt and rejection. You may not understand why the other is behaving this way and are baffled as to why they are showing such loathing towards you. Whether they try to hide their feelings or not, you still sense their hidden animosity, and it does not feel good!

Most Empaths blame themselves if they get rejected by another. They may tell themselves they are not friendly enough, nice enough or good enough for those who spurned them. But this could not be further from the truth. Through observations and contemplations, I discovered three main reasons why people cool off or take an instant dislike to the balanced Empath:

1. **The Empath acts as a mirror**
2. **The Empath's vibration is too fast**
3. **The Empath's stillness is inaccurately read**

The Mirror Effect

One reason people may cold-shoulder them, is because the Empath reflects to them their shortcomings and truths. In a bid to hide their truth, it is common for people to act in an inauthentic way. They pretend to be something they are not because they do not like aspects of their personality. They may be insecure, carry deep shame, or be hiding a trait they do not believe will be accepted. On the darker side of the spectrum, some hide aspects of their personality to manipulate others. But, as a whole, the majority of people, who put on an act, do so to find acceptance.

The fear of being judged or disliked, for what they don't like about themselves, makes some people act inauthentically. They wear a mask and pretend to be something they are not. Even Empaths put on a face when out in the world. There are some, however, who never remove their mask and go through life with a false identity. But when they come face-to-face with an Empath there is no hiding from these concealed traits. The mask comes off and their truth displayed in full view. Aspects of their personality, they worked so hard to hide or deny, are mirrored and waved in their face. This invariably causes a fury and a backlash directed towards the Empath. They are being shown, what they consider to be, their shortcomings and it does not feel good.

Because being around an Empath may arouse uncomfortable truths, for some, it can initiate a keen loathing. What those experiencing this loathing may not realize is the intense dislike they have, towards the Empath, is actually a reflection of themselves (This can also be experienced by the Empath who has not faced their truth). The truth of who they are is revealed. Anything hidden becomes seen within the "**Mirror of an Empath**".

Some Empaths pick up on other people's emotions, hidden behaviors and true personality traits, and inadvertently project them back. They wear other people's truths like the mask they hide behind. But they are mostly unaware they have this ability. In the days before they knew they were an Empath, they may have mistaken the insecurities of others as their own.

If someone has characteristics, they don't like about themselves, they are reminded of them when in an Empath's presence. Traits such as: jealousy, anger, hatred, feeling unworthy, low self-esteem and self-grandeur are all mirrored back by an Empath. This is one reason why instant dislikes, towards the Empath, are formed. If someone is off with you, it could be you are reflecting back to them the truth they deny. Or there could be another reason...

Vibrating Too Fast

Just like an Empath dislikes being around people who spew negativity, some people cannot stand to be around clean positive energy. When you work on yourself, and positively change your mind, body or spirit, you become cleaner and purer, and thus your vibration increases. This can be the cause of a rejection from those more comfortable with low-level energy.

In the past, I noticed when I was in a low emotional place some seemed to prefer me that way. But when I changed myself, transformed my life, and put myself in a high vibrating space, those same people didn't like it. I felt like they wanted to bring me back down. They did this in many ways: snide comments, ridiculing my discoveries, or new ways of being, even attacking me. The sad thing is they were unaware they were doing it. Had I confronted them, about their behaviour, they would have denied it.

Vibrating in a higher space can make you repel even those you love. People sense change; whether it is visually apparent or not, and they subconsciously notice when another has increased their frequency. Because you don't feel like a fit to them anymore, as your vibration no longer matches theirs, people you have known well may suddenly become cruel or hostile towards you, in their bid to bring you down. Not everyone is ready to raise their vibration. Some may still have lessons to learn, at their frequency level, and are not ready to move up. And because they are not ready to move onwards and upwards, they may try to pull you back down to their level.

Your Stillness is Inaccurately Read

To those of an insecure nature, your quiet and sometimes distant Empath ways may be seen as a sign of disrespect or a snub. When they are overwhelmed, Empaths often appear aloof and some may class this as arrogant or superior behavior. Normally, when an Empath acts in an aloof or distant way, it is because they are on overload. Having taken on too much stimuli, from their surroundings and in serious need of recharging, the Empath wants nothing more than to be invisible to others. When on overload, and heading towards a fatigue meltdown, the last thing they can deal with is someone offloading their troubles, like so many do. Even polite conversation is too much to bear. This is often seen as a rejection, or an insult, to those you are quiet towards. The last thing an Empath wants is for others to think they are snobby, or in any way better, but, sadly, their still and withdrawn ways are often mistaken as superiority.

Because others don't feel what an Empath does, it is difficult for them to understand why they act the way they do. Sadly, the more angst-ridden someone is, the more they will be offended by your quiet ways and the more likely they are to verbally or mentally attack you.

Random dislikes towards the Empath is part of life. No one can control what others think of them. As long as you are being the best person you can be that is all that matters Always remember to stay true to yourself and don't act in inauthentic ways just to please others. Whatever you do people will judge you so you may as well please yourself first.

Reacting to society's thoughts and judgments will hold you back from your true path. To be aware as an Empath you need to understand how the judgments of others affect you.

Being Judged

Have you ever wondered why you choose not to reveal all you know and feel to others? Perhaps you believe they will not understand you or maybe you feel they will judge you negatively?

The energy emitted from judgments is dark and sticky and is awful to experience. Empaths know when they are being judged. It is sensed powerfully. And, because they don't want to give others the opportunity to judge, and reject them, they often keep to themselves what they think, feel and know.

Empaths are life's observers! They watch, notice, and see things others don't. Being an observer is not the same as being a judger. When you observe, you do so from a perspective of learning and understanding. When someone judges, it is often because they believe they are superior or they are mentally putting another down.

In common society, you are expected to act and behave in a certain way. If you don't fit into the expected mold you are often judged. The problem with that is Empaths do not want to fit in. They want to follow their truth, find their purpose and live the life that fits them. They know being fulfilled and following their true purpose and passion is what life is all about. They also know living this way can lead to being judged, for not fitting in, which is often followed by rejection.

To avoid the dreadful energy of judgment, a number of Empaths may comply and fit in with what is expected. In doing so, they avoid the path they are meant to follow. If this happens it will cause the Empath depression and unhappiness.

Society judges everyone for everything: Attractiveness, size, fashion-sense, wealth, social status, career, living location, race and beliefs. This is a world where being different, or having individualist ideals, is frowned upon. Some may pretend to celebrate individuality whilst secretly following the herd! The Fear of judgment stops anyone moving forward. It can imprison you into a life you have either long-since outgrown or never fitted in with in the first place. The whole purpose of your existence is to evolve. Evolvement happens through experiences and the knowledge you gain, your self-betterment and your happiness. You are not here to follow other people's ideals and standards; but you are here to discover your own and to develop as souls. This is done this by following the truth and not the herd.

Fear of judgment is a seed planted early in life, as a way to control and divide, but realizing this is halfway to overcoming it. On your path to evolvement, you need to remember you are not what other people think of you. That belief is limiting and will only hold you back. You are here to be free. Free to be yourself and free to the enjoy life for which you are destined. You are not here to follow the herd and spend your life in fear of being judged. Don't let someone else's judgments dictate to you what your path should be.

It is a known fact that the Sensitive dislike criticism. They are affected by it more than most. If you too are overly sensitive just remember: this is your journey and what you chose to do or learn is for your growth! When you are on the right path, following your heart's passions and purpose, doors will open. Those who judge or criticize you are not in a good place. They are often the unhappiest of people. They themselves fear being judged and for that reason they become the predator instead of the prey.

People can criticize you but it doesn't make them right! If someone judges you, you do not need get them to see things from your perspective. It is not your place to change another's opinion of you. That is their job. It may be hurtful, but don't allow it to stop you from **Be**ing who you are. If you know in your heart you always act with integrity, and are the best version of yourself, then that is good enough.

Inauthenticity and Why It Feels So Bad

Ever spent time with someone who, on the surface, seem as nice as pie but when with them you feel awful and struggle to form a sentence? This is a caused by your Empathic antenna sensing all is not what it seems. You are detecting that they are showing a fake persona.

When an Empath comes across phony people it is common for them to shut down. They are protecting themselves from taking on, what they feel is, negative energy. This can be seen as stumbling over their words or their memory and thought process being affected. Their brain gets scrambled. Anyone who is not emanating truthful vibes will put an Empath on high alert.

In my days as a hairdresser, I never understood why when I was with certain clients I would get such awful trepidations. It was only when I discovered I was an Empath that it all made sense. I was feeling their pain, or hidden aspects of their personality, which they were hiding in inauthentic behavior.

A cheerful smile and an upbeat demeanor may suggest a happy person, but if it is not the truth an Empath will feel it as discomfort. This is not to say those who are inauthentic are bad people. It is often the kindest or broken people who put on an act. Most times, those who care about others do not want to bring them down, by showing their true feelings, and instead cover them up with pleasantries.

There are many levels of inauthenticity and many reasons for it. In the early days of discovering of one's Empath abilities it may not always be easy to pinpoint why someone feels so bad. Here are some behaviors that may leave you feeling uncomfortable:

- Someone who fears rejection but acts overly nice to get adoration.
- Someone filled with hate or anger working hard to convince you otherwise.
- Someone insecure, damaged by a destructive childhood, playing the tough guy.
- Someone who has built a new personality to hide the person they believe won't be accepted by society.
- Someone who is full of insincere praise for others.
- Someone making up stories to make themselves sound interesting

And this is how you may react:

- Avoiding being in their presence, yet not having a valid reason to do so (they did not say or do anything to hurt you).
- Not being able to talk to them. Sentences won't form in your mouth. Your brain acts like you have no memory.

You only ask questions. If you talk it feels like it makes no sense.

- Having a sense of dread in the pit of stomach that won't go until you are no longer in said person's presence.
- Any more than an hour spent in their company will drain you and leave you feeling ill.
- Feeling guilt, you may like the person but dislike how it feels to be with them.
- Feeling helpless around them.

Just because an Empath feels untruths in another does not mean they do not act fake themselves. For some, when they feel uneasy around a pretender, it may mean they are picking up a trait they dislike about themselves which they too hide from the world.

Some of the people who affect and Empath in the most debilitating of ways are those who embody narcissistic traits.

The Narcissist and the Empath

Empaths often find themselves on the radar of those with a narcissistic nature. Where you find an Empath, you will find a narcissist nearby. There are many reasons for this. I believe one being Nature's way of creating balance. In the Empath, there is too much empathy and in the narcissist, too little. To create balance, Nature brings the two together.

Those with strengths in a certain area will often be paired with those who have weakness. You are then supposed to work together to find equilibrium. But, the problem many face is they haven't been shown how to do this. They are thrown in at the deep end and left to figure it out for themselves.

Instead of trying to rationalize, or understand, the reasons behind people's behavior, society teaches the populace to attack those who hurt them, or those who are deemed to be a threat. This way of being just puts people at loggerheads.

It is an inbuilt trait of an Empath to see life from all perspectives and to empathize with others. They often stay quiet about issues, or put up with bad behavior, in order to be the peacekeeper. But if continually taken advantage of they eventually snap. If someone repeatedly behaves in a cruel or selfish manner, the Empath will react. And if this involves a run-in with a narcissist it never normally ends well.

There is generally a no-win situation when going up against a narcissist. They lie, cheat, see everything only from their perspective and then lie some more. The only way to win is to not get involved and walk away. Empaths often learn this the hard way after being burnt or watching others get burnt.

The dynamics of a narcissist and an Empath can prove to be a unique contradiction. They may have a natural aversion and an equal attraction. Some say they are two sides of the same coin. I would certainly agree that an Empath and narcissist have heightened levels of sensitivity but it is expressed in opposite ways.

The Empath's sensitive side causes them to feel strong emotional pain and they get hurt easily. But it also contributes to their consideration, fierce loyalty and their abundance of empathy for others.

The narcissist's sensitivities also contribute to their emotional pain and getting offended. But, in most cases, their pain has made them bitter, resentful and vengeful. They have no empathy and when they have been offended it is often caused by a wounded ego as opposed to a pained soul (as in the Empath's case).

The push and pull between an Empath and a narcissist is a palpable contradiction. It is as though there is a repelling magnetism between them. They can have a natural aversion and an equal attraction. Empaths have no tolerance of narcissistic uncaring behavior; especially when it is directed at others or to the underdog. But they can still fall under the spell of a narcissist.

The origin of narcissism stems from the myth of Narcissus, the youth from ancient Greece who fell in love with his own reflection in the water, only to drown. The definition is: A psychological condition characterized by self-preoccupation and high self-esteem with a distinct lack of empathy, and having an excessive love or admiration of oneself.

Narcissists see themselves as important and deserving, they also believe they are more attractive than most. They have big egos which they expect others to pander to. They pay special attention to their appearance and constantly polish and refine themselves. A narcissist cannot pass a mirror without taking a look and they will be seen taking endless selfies on their phone. Narcissists see everyone as being inferior to them and have no empathy.

Insults to others are part of the narcissist's way. They think nothing of putting other people down and judging them for what they consider flaws. But if anyone criticizes, or challenges their own behaviour, they lash out. They see themselves as perfect, with no flaws and act aggressively towards anyone who may suggest otherwise.

Because they see themselves as more important, narcissists will take advantage of others, especially the Empath, and act manipulatively towards them. Using tactics such as fake flattery to get them to do their dirty work. They often target the Empaths because of their kind-hearted nature.

Many people exhibit mild forms or narcissism. Modern society breeds it. Narcissism can range from healthy to pathological. It is known that narcissism is a cover for vulnerability or personal inadequacy. Narcissists build a wall of defense for their own protection. They insult others as a way to feel better about themselves and to prevent others from noticing their flaws. These types would be labeled as vulnerable narcissists. Deep down they want nothing more than to be liked and accepted.

Some Empaths may be drawn to the vulnerable narcissists because they feel the damage and pain they hide from the world.

An Empath may be drawn into a relationship with a narcissist because they want to heal or nurture the wounds carried by the narcissist. The attraction is often mutual and a narcissist will be drawn to the Empath because of their unique ability to listen and nurture. An Empath can make the narcissist feel empowered by their devout loyalty and caring ways.

But not all narcissism results from being insecure. There is another type known as grandiose narcissism. This narcissism is pathological and stems from a person's belief of being better than everyone else and comes with an untouchable ego. This is going to the far end of the spectrum of narcissism. These types believe they are god-like and will see others only as an extension of themselves. It is their belief that others are there purely to serve them.

The grandiose believe in their own greatness and consider no one as a match to them. These types often work their way into positions of power. They use the law of attraction without even realizing they are doing it. Because they believe so much in their own superiority and magnificence, they draw to them a fantastical life. This is why you will see many grandiose narcissists as politicians, celebrities or powerful business people. Once in positions of power the grandiose narcissist will surround themselves with yes-men who cater to their every need. And because of this they grow to become even more monster-like.

There is a strong division between Empaths and their draw to narcissists. It should be pointed out here that not all of them will be attracted in any which way. Some Empaths will be drawn to the vulnerable narcissist like a moth to a flame. Other Empaths run to the hills at the first sniff of narcissism, because the last thing they have energy for is a needy, sensitive person. An Empath may be pulled towards the grandiose narcissist because they are very "un-needy" and often want little emotional nourishment. Because they have such little emotion, they may feel almost clean to an Empath.

Any Empath who has fallen in love with a narcissist will find their safety switches turned off. They can become blinded to their own intuition that warns them of unacceptable behavior. The narcissist can make anyone believe they are at fault and they never accept responsibility for their actions. Even if they end up apologizing, they will still lay the blame elsewhere. This just adds to the Empath's burden.

A relationship with a narcissist often does much damage to the Empath's psyche. It can create or add to insecurities and self-doubts. It would be pointless to say avoid this kind of relationship because that is not the way life works. You often only realize what type of relationship you are in many months or years into it. On the plus-side there is much to learn from bad relationships. If a relationship weakens you, you eventually grow strength from it. When you understand, and accept, the reason you were drawn into the bad relationship you gain power from it. This in turn stops others from being able to take advantage of you. Not that you become hardened, it just becomes clear your strings can no longer be pulled. Transformation always happens when you go through the darkest of challenges.

The hurdle many Empaths need to overcome is learning to stop accepting the blame for other people's bad behavior. And not to feel guilty when saying no! Blame is pointless! You either live with another's way or you don't and you either accept someone for who they are or you don't. No one wins when the blame card is put on the table, not the Empath or the narcissist, you just lose the opportunity for growth.

Any damage that arises from a bad relationship or friendship, whether with a narcissist or not, dissolves the moment you understand why you were drawn into the situation in the first place. If you are left feeling empty and vulnerable you may simply need more time to heal or you may have other buried issues which need addressing

Feeling Empty

Because Empaths carry other people's emotions, pains, ideas and beliefs it can leave them feeling empty and disconnected from their true-self. They may then end up living a life that isn't based on their true desires. This emptiness, or void, can also be a direct result of carrying too much emotional pain and having many buried insecurities.

Part of an Empaths path to an empowered transformation is about discovering what weakens them. You have to know your vulnerabilities, and what caused them, before you can transform your life. You need a firm foundation before you can build yourself up, and this involves knowing the origins of your insecurities. Which takes us to the next Secret…

Secret 4

How Past Insecurities Impact the Empath

Once you become aware of being an Empath everything about life starts to makes sense. It becomes clear why you have sensed all you have and why you have always felt so different from others. This knowledge alone sets you off on a new path and onto the journey of discovering "all things energy".

One of the first steps of an Empath's voyage to transformation is learning to differentiate between their energy and that which belongs to others. When you understand this, you are a step closer to reclaiming your personal power. This in turn enables you to block foreign energies, not belonging to you, and take measures to prevent psychic attack. But, before an Empath can allow for total transformation, finding overall balance and stability, they need to understand how they were affected by their past.

All past encounters, good and bad, have shaped the Empath you are today. Any pain or suffering you experienced has contributed to your strengths or weaknesses. Your strengths do not pose a problem, it is your weaknesses that need to be addressed. To overcome any insecurities or nonsensical emotional issues, you may have, you first need to discover their origin. The aim of this Secret is to do just that.

The Empath's Path of Pain

If someone were to endure the equivalent in physical pain the Empath experiences in emotions, they would be hailed as a brave hero. Yet this is a far cry from how most Empaths see themselves.

Most Empaths have faced many hardships and battles in their lives and they have learnt a lot from them. They often make their most valuable of discoveries, and life lessons, the hard way. Many of which happened in childhood or young adult years.

As they late Michael Jackson would often say: 'We are all a product of our childhood!' This basically means what you experienced in your childhood will determine your future.

Finding Your Pain

Most remember a painful event, from their past, that has shaped them into who they are today. But there are many more experiences, you may not remember, responsible for scripting your life. You may be a product of your childhood but, as an Empath, you are also an accumulation of your close friends' and family's problems and insecurities.

Childhood was a baffling time for most Empaths. Even back then they knew they were different. They had an outlook on life others didn't and were often left bewildered by the cruel behaviour, seen as being normal, in other children.

Children may be innocent but they can be unkind and peevish. Their foolish, naive words were often declared without any consideration of their consequence and they always caused damage to those they were inflicted upon. No more so than to the Sensitive child.

I remember a popular rhyme that was sang in times of petty playground squabbles which always left me scratching my head: *'Sticks and stones will break my bones but words will never hurt me!'* As a child, I remember thinking this rhyme was not true. Nasty, hateful words did so much more damage than sticks or stones. People healed from being struck, by a rock or stick, but words caused lasting pain.

Even if they had the most idyllic of childhoods, most Empaths carry wounds from spiteful words said to them in the early years. Whether they remember the words or not, the hurt is still carried through life. All children were damaged by cruel words but those who are Sensitive were destroyed by them. Because they did not know how to deal with the pain that came with them, many Empaths pretended that they were unaffected by their childhood traumas, often burying the memories. But, sadly, the denied wounds of youth do not heal. Buried emotional pain just lays the foundations for more to be built.

Both good and bad childhood experiences are reflected in adults. For example: if a child is brought up in a strong, supportive and loving environment this is seen in their own positive, loving way. If a child is exposed to anger, stress or anxiety—even if there was a lot of love in the home—they too will carry this with them. For the Empath, however, what they experienced in those early years is amplified in adulthood because of the way they process and store painful emotion.

Some children seem resilient to angry outbursts. Parents' arguing is one such example. But just because a child seems unaffected by violent arguments does not mean it won't cause lasting damage. Anger energy is stored within the cells and within the energy field. It affects the functioning of the brain and the way the hormones work. Anger experienced in an Empath's childhood, will act as a trauma trigger for many years to come. Any future outbursts, they witness, will ignite the memory of a past incident and the fear that may have gone with it.

Everyone has at least one memory of a nasty argument from childhood. Like many children, I witnessed my parents arguing. Parents' arguments are hard enough for any child to endure, but for a Sensitive child it is extra painful. I remember the intense emotional pain I felt as my parents hurled insults at each other.

I would cry and beg them to stop fighting but my cries always fell on deaf ears. They were both filled with too much anger to realize what damage they were doing. Their only interest was proving the other wrong. I also remember not understanding why my three sisters were not reacting the same way. I knew they didn't like my parents' arguments but they were clearly not as affected or sensing the hurt I was. Back then, I was not aware I was feeling my parents' anguish and hurt emotions, as they argued, as well as my own discomfort. It was only as an adult Empath I came to understand why I felt so bad when they argued.

I do not blame my parents for arguing in front of me. I know and understand the human condition too well. We all go through tough times in life and lash out (especially in mid-life).

Most do not know how to channel their pain or uncover its cause. And instead of processing it, they often end up lashing out at those they love the most. When people don't understand their pain, they have to find something, or someone, to blame it on and that is often those who they see every day. Anger, or inner-hurt, can blind anyone to the truth of a situation and indeed to the inconsiderateness of their own actions and words.

If, as a child, you were caught up in any type of conflict, whether it was aimed at you or not, it has more impact on your current life situation than you probably know. For example: you may fear confrontation for the fear of an argument or loud voices may make you anxious. If in your past, raised voices meant an argument, or punishment, they will invariably be the cause of a trauma reaction today. Any raised voices, even from strangers, can ignite inner-fear. You may also overreact if someone behaves angrily towards you. Your emotional memory tells you that any loud voices means an angry conflict is on its way (as was the case in childhood).

If you look at any insecurity you have you often find its roots planted in the early years. Childhood was the time the seeds of insecurity were sewn. It was the breeding ground for many of your present emotional pains. The teen years also play a part in sparking adult insecurities.

Teenage Years

The adult Empath's anxieties can stem from several aspects of teenage life. For example: being on the receiving end of ridicule, or intimidation, can cause deep emotional wounds they carry with them through life, as can acts of betrayal or disloyalty from trusted friends and family.

A major cause of an Empath's teenage angsts is due to hormonal changes. As they go from being a child into early adulthood, it is part of all teenagers' life to go through an upheaval in their emotional state. Hormones play havoc with moods and are behind many unsavory behaviors. This shift in hormones can be a huge turning point for the Empath as their emotions, and insecurities, take on a life of their own.

As their social fears climb to new heights, teenage Empaths have a lot of life-changing "stuff" to deal with. Teenage insecurities are a challenge for anyone to endure, but for those who experience the emotions of others, life becomes a theater of nightmares. Because they pick up on other people's insecurities, and unknowingly take them on as their own, the teen Empath carries a great deal of emotional debris. The fact they spend so much time with other teenagers, also in the throes of hormonal change, makes early adulthood a turbulently trying time. To the unknowing Empath, emotions and insecurities have the same vibration whomever they belong to. In teenage years, when they have never experienced these feelings before, it is difficult for them to discern between their insecurities and others'.

The teen years cause an Empath so much confusion and disruption that they unwittingly acquire traits, or insecurities, that do not belong to them. They may become shy, self-doubting or nervous just by spending too much time around other adolescents who own those fears. Spend enough time around anyone who has social fear (typical of teenagers) and those traits will become embedded in the unaware Empath's psyche. Collecting personality traits, such as issues, worries or doubts, is a common theme for the Empath teen. These fears will then shape their future.

High school is the perfect breeding ground for insecurities to take root by the way of emotional contagion. Spending time around lots of juveniles, with heightened energy and emotions, puts the Empath at risk of contamination. The insecurities, picked up from others, pollutes their own personality which may then last for many years into their future. In fact, this personality pollution often lasts until it is recognized. If an Empath has involuntarily claimed the traits of others, as their own, it will make them feel like they are living a lie.

Unaware Empaths rarely understand why they feel all they do when they enter early adulthood. Spending time in group gatherings can be an uncomfortable affair as they are bombarded with a deluge of amplified emotions. Because they unwittingly take on the views and feelings of other "mixed-up" adolescents, they may come to claim them as their own.

In their bid to block out all this crazy insecure energy, and to help them fit in, many teenage Empaths turn to alcohol. Not realizing alcohol only makes their symptoms worse.

When I look back on my young adulthood years I can see why I experienced all I did. I now understand why certain situations made me so uncomfortable. In taking on the emotions and insecurities, I mistook for my own, I had no idea I was both reading and absorbing the energy of others. I thought it was my own shyness that made me feel all those strange inexplicable emotions.

If you suspect you may have acquired personality traits from others, in adolescence, you need to take a peep into your own childhood. If, for example, you were not a shy child but suddenly developed shyness in teenage years, look at the friends you had. Were they shy or insecure? Do you think you could have latched onto their insecurities and adapted them into your personality? This is not to say you can blame all your social hang-ups on other people, everyone has weaknesses to deal with, but if you experience unfathomable insecurities, or fears, it is wise to question their origin. Understanding how many insecurities you have lifted from others, or taken from your past, is the key to overcoming them.

Another teenage angst, that affects many young Empaths, is being ignored. Empaths are excellent listeners and do so on many levels. They hear and they care what others have to say, this is even obvious in their teenage years. Sadly, not everyone has this gift. Some people, especially teenagers and young adults, are only interested in themselves and what they want to talk about. When having a conversation, they are not always listening to what is being said but rather waiting for their chance to talk. No one knows they are not listening so no harm is caused… except some people do. The unaware teenage Empath can sense when they are not being listened to, which can lead them into believing what they say holds no interest to others. If they spend a lot of time around those who don't listen, they may believe their conversation is uninteresting. This can then create a phobia of talking.

Because Empaths are listeners, it can make people want to over-talk when in their presence. Whether the Empath has something of interest to say or not, may not matter to the other person, having the captive audience of such an avid listener is enough to put anyone on a roll. When people do not listen, it doesn't always mean they are more interested in what they have to say, sometimes it is because being truly listened to, and heard, is like a drug. This is often why an Empath does not get chance to speak. But sadly, the young, impressionable Empath does not always know this.

Many Empaths carry insecurity stemming from their past, especially childhood and the teenage years, it is part of who they are. However, recognizing where it comes from is important to letting it go. Knowing what triggers emotional pain can be enough to help switch it off.

So far, I may have painted a picture that may show an Empath as being a quiet victim in their teen years, but for some that was not the case. Empaths are incredibly intelligent beings who will adapt for their own survival. If their emotional pain, or fears, became overwhelming, some Sensitive teens built a defensive barrier and put on a show of bravado, often acting in bullyish ways to keep others away. This is a self-defence coping mechanism. To protect themselves from bullies, or spiteful people, the Empath may morph into the hunter. Teenagers quickly learn it is better to be the hunter than the hunted and this is the reason some Empaths pretended to be tougher than they actually feel (Empaths are also good actors), to scare potential tormenters away. If, in their teenage actions, they caused hurt to anyone they carry the shame and guilt of it into adulthood. I suppose this is a form of self-inflicted karma. They hold the shame and pain, they inflicted on others, until they forgive themselves or apologize for their past actions.

Rejection, Loyalty and Betrayal

Another cause of deep-set insecurities within the Empath comes from rejection and betrayal. Both of which open wounds so deep they may not heal, even after the memory has long-since faded. Being rejected is part of life for every human being; for the Empath, however, it cuts far deeper than most.

Your first rejection was probably experienced in childhood from a friend or sibling. Most will have some memory of an early rejection and it was likely the foundation for more insecurities to be built.

The reason it cuts the Empath so deeply is because rejection is a form of betrayal. Empaths are very loyal to those they allow in their small circle and, whether from family or friends, they need that loyalty to be a two-way street. But this is a dog-eat-dog world. Most people have little in the way of empathy towards others. And just because someone has the same blood running through their veins, does not mean they will have the same understanding. The significance of loyalty can hold very different meanings for everyone. The following passage will strike a chord even to those who are not Sensitive:

'Life has taught me that you can't control someone's loyalty. No matter how good you are to them, doesn't mean they'll treat you the same. No matter how much they mean to you, doesn't mean they'll value you the same. Sometimes the people you love the most, turn out to be the people you can trust the least.'

-    *Trent Shelton*

If you were born as an Empath, you are a minority. Few will even get close to feeling what you do, they do not have the capacity. Most Empaths come to learn they cannot expect others to change their ways, they can only change themselves and how they deal with rejection, disloyalty and betrayal.

For the Empath, loyalty and trust is an essential part of life. It is an unwritten law. For most, loyalty was learnt at a young age, from family or friends, but for the Empath they were born with a strong sense of loyalty and it is part of their genetic make-up. If someone hurts or is disloyal towards an Empath, they may expect their family and friends (those they are loyal towards) to be supportive. They hope they will have their back and be empathetic towards their plight. If this does not happen, or if they act as sympathizers towards those who have hurt them, the Empath will see this betrayal.

The sourness of rejection, betrayal and disloyalty, slowly eats away at the Empath. Subsequent betrayals will feed the previous and the pain associated with them increases. This pain causes weakness and only serves in attracting more of the same (like attracts like). Meaning, you will draw more people and situations that lead to betrayal and rejection.

Disloyalty, or rejection, does not have to be anything murderous. It can be as simple as someone repeatedly breaking a date. Everyone knows what it feels like to be, in any way, let down, not good. Empaths often go out of their way not to do this. When it is not reciprocated, it may be taken as rejection. When you make plans, you have made an agreement. If the plans are broken, due to unforeseen circumstances, this is not a problem for the Empath. But when they are let down by a lie, or a weak excuse, it is seen as an insult or a snub. Because an Empath knows when they are being lied to, if someone breaks a date with an untruth, it is seen as an act of disloyalty.

We live in a society where lies are quietly seen as acceptable. People behave like there are no repercussions for telling lies, taking advantage of others, or being overtly disrespectful. Not true! What goes around comes around. Everyone is responsible for their own actions. Just because the few see it as being okay to treat people badly, does not make it right. Some people tell themselves it is ok to tell lies, or treat others badly, but we should all treat others how we want to be treated ourselves.

Shadow-Side

If past demons, or insecurities, are not faced they grow and eventually become something which is known as the shadow-side. Your shadow-side is an aspect of yourself which normally ignites shame or insecurity. It could be an emotional attribute that makes you uncomfortable, something you were ridiculed for in youth, or an accumulation of many things. But whatever it is, if you do not face your shadow-side it will get darker and more destructive. And, for this reason, it is important to uncover any hidden traits or buried pain. Whilst you bury a side of yourself, for whatever reason, you will never be happy or feel complete.

Before you can face your buried issues, you need to know what they are. This is where looking into your past helps. If you do not know the root-cause of your buried insecurities, or what your shadow-side even looks like, it is difficult to face them. (I must point out at this stage that some fears and insecurities, which are mistaken for the shadow-side, are in fact caused by being out-of-balance—chakras out of alignment, food intolerances, or being ungrounded, etc.—but more on that later.)

One of the biggest causes of unhappiness on this planet is people not knowing themselves. When you hide a side of yourself, without knowing the reason, it will not only cause spiritual and emotional pain, but it will weaken your physical and energetic bodies.

Hate, anger, jealousy and fear of rejection are four traits associated most with the shadow-side. Because it is known how destructive they are, these are the attributes most Empaths bury. You may hate someone for the way they behaved towards you. Anger may be inherited from an angry parent. Praise and attention given to a childhood friend, or sibling, may lead to a jealous streak. And being rejected as a child, by an unknowing parent for instance, may have caused an intense fear of rejection. All simple and innocent triggers, but all of which can snowball. And lead to deep-set insecurities.

You also have to consider that some of the traits, you hide from others, may have been inherited or stem from a past life. But even if you were born into them, and they were not caused by some traumatic life event or from being a bad person, you still need to face them. Wherever they originated, it is important to uncover your shadow-side and hidden secrets. And if they can't be released, accept and learn to live with them.

If you are currently experiencing more anguish than normal it is a good time to check your back-story and find out to what these issues link. When checking your back story, the first place you need to check in with is your intuition. What is it telling you?

An Empath's intuition is always an excellent guide. You just need to ask the right questions. If it tells you your emotional pain stems from a rejection, or an injustice in childhood, it is time to let it go. Because of the time factor, it is difficult to know what your original hurt was. Sometimes, early issues are actually quite minor but have been allowed to snowball. Over the years, hidden pain escalates and attaches more associated pains to it. When I say associated pain, I mean those similar in nature.

Sensitive people bury negative traits because they know how destructive they are. But burying them does not lose them. They always show up and cause damage. Often, when you simply recognize and accept these attributes they lose their hold on you.

The world is now in a state of flux and because of this people are in crisis, especially the Empaths. People are having their unresolved matters coming up because they need to be cleared. Now is the time for everyone to face their shadow-sides and hidden issues! Unfortunately, many are choosing not to do this. Instead they are projecting blame for their emotions onto others which is another blow for the Empaths of the world. Not only because they feel this unresolved energy, powerfully, but because they often end up in its firing line. This may also ignite a traumatic response.

Empath Trauma Triggers

If you have someone in your life who acts as a trauma trigger, they will have no-doubt sprung to mind upon reading this sentence. Those who act as a trauma trigger incite a reaction at the mere mention of their name. An Empath may become awash with painful emotions, just by thinking about this certain person. This reaction is caused by a response within the brain. If someone caused you emotional pain in the past, the amygdala, in the brain, will perceive them as a threat and will then send a provoking emotional response to warn you of this danger. This response is normally felt as an overwhelming sense of dread or other negative emotion. It is often followed by the release of the fight-or-flight hormones, cortisol and adrenalin, which fuels up your energy. This reaction would be beneficial if there was a flesh-eating zombie chasing you, as you would have the energy to run away or stay and fight it. But because these hormones do not get used, you are often left in an anxious state after experiencing a trauma trigger. This will further incite any future traumatic responses in regards to said person.

For the Empath, feeling other people's energy and emotions is normal, both negative and positive. But if someone lives under a constant cloud of negative energy, and are riddled with angsts, they too can become a trauma trigger for the Empath. These people, who think nothing of spewing out their dark angry emotions, often refuse to accept or change their behavior. Even when it has been pointed out to them how their actions affect others, they still refuse to change. They find fault in everyone and choose not to see the good qualities in those around them. Because they have such dark energy, which is incompatible with an Empath, the memory of them acts as a trauma trigger

Anyone can become a trauma trigger to the Empath, but they will normally be a family member, friend, employer or teacher, etc. The very thought of them can suck the joy out of life just like the Dementors in the Harry Potter books. If you have had a bad experience with a trauma trigger person in the past, even if it was just taking on their insidious energy, it often means they will create distress for you in the future.

If you are a calm and peaceful person, as most Empaths are, these trauma trigger people feel like poison and are responsible for activating anything from dread to anxiety. Their energy can even make you feel physically ill. It doesn't matter how long it is since you last saw them either; if they regularly caused you painful or uncomfortable emotions, in the past, you will be triggered even after a length of time has passed.

It has to be said, it is not always negative people who cause painful responses and thus become trauma triggers. Anyone who is suffering emotionally can activate the Empath's pain body. This happens when their pain is something to which you relate.

If, for example, you have suffered bereavement, being around the recently bereaved can act as a trauma trigger. Feeling their hurt can take you back to your own time of loss and activate those emotional memories.

Trauma Trigger or Psychic Attack?

People can be behind both a psychic attack and act as a traumatic trigger. Psychic attacks come out of the blue. When they happen, you feel the negative vibes sent, mentally, by a certain person. A trauma response happens when the person, acting as a trigger, is mentioned in conversation, seen from a distance or something sparks a memory of them. Every time said person comes into your energy field, through thought, word or presence it can be enough to activate you. You may be able to avoid trauma trigger people but you cannot always stop them from mentally connecting. The best way to stop a mental connection, from a trauma trigger person, is to use the same technique you use when taking on other people's thoughts or emotions.

If you suspect a trauma triggers' mental energy is connecting with your own, repeat this line, in your head or out loud: 'If this energy is not mine go back to where you came.' Once you feel it recede, distract yourself.

The Enigma of the Empath

Empaths are an enigma! There will always be those who feel uncomfortable with their stillness and quiet mystery. Some people attack what they don't understand. Empaths know when others speak ill of them, they can feel the energy of low-vibrational words being used against them. All thoughts and words are energy. If someone makes unkind remarks against them, even behind their back, the Empath feels the intention of those words.

Verbal attacks or ill thoughts, directed towards the Empath, may ignite the insecurity of not being good enough. But, believe me when I say, if you are an Empath you are more than good enough!

One thing I have learnt on this journey, as an Empath, is that there is no point trying to show others who we are. People see and hear only what they want to see and hear; especially when they are not yet "awake".

There is little point trying to get another to see things from your perspective, it is a waste of your valuable energy. By defending your nature, to those who do not have the same emotional intelligence, it ends up causing you more pain and frustration.

People don't always understand the Empaths and it is for this reason they may get criticized or rejected. Empaths are a simply a rare and unique breed who do things differently and feel things most could not imagine. Those who reject or criticize the Empath will probably never understand them. They can't because they don't possess the same emotional intelligence. That is not to be critical of those who don't understand the Empaths of the world. Each person is on a unique journey. Even those who do bad things can offer valuable lessons to those who work to make the world a better place.

The good thing with insecurities, stemming from you past, is they can be overcome. One of the first ways to do this is to accept them. Truthful acceptance is a gigantic step towards emotional freedom.

Here are some ways of finding acceptance:

- Accept that you are rare and unique. Others may not always understand you but that is ok.

- Accept that feeling pain, from betrayal or disloyalty, is part of the voyage of an Empath. There is no point fighting it. It is what is and know your pain is serving a higher purpose.

- Accept that people see only what they want and are ready to see. Not everyone can question their behavior. If it is part of their life-plan they will eventually learn.

- Accept all the pain you experience, as an outcome of other people's actions, is happening for a reason. To build inner-strength.

- Accept it is your responsibility to ease your pain. You do this by taking the steps to stay in balance and avoid anything that brings you down. If getting in balance means avoiding certain people who drain your energy or fill you with negativity, that is what you must do (see Secret 7).

Know yourself and understand your true value. Love and believe in yourself. You are here to help change the world. The betrayal and rejection you experience is a just part of your amazing journey. You may not be able to see it now but you will one day. Acceptance offers the key to seeing this!

Find the Answers

Discovery and acceptance goes a long way to freeing the Empath of insecurities and emotional pain. However, there are other contributing factors that means an Empath may experience unnecessary emotional pain and anxiety. We will learn about this a little later, but for now we will move onto our next Secret and uncover how to find your true path.

Secret 5

Find Your Empath Wings

One thing I know for sure is the Empaths are here for an important reason. I can feel it. As I'm sure you can too. You may not know what this purpose is yet, but you are certainly on your way to finding out.

You were born Sensitive for a reason. Not as a punishment but as a way to build an emotional strength and an empathic understanding not seen on this planet for an age. Your empathy, intuition and all-encompassing emotions have already thrust you upon a challenging road. This road has taken you on many highs and lows and you have learnt a lot. You've experienced a world's worth of emotions and pain... A fact few can lay claim to.

Once you understand the root cause of your imbalances, and overcome them, it frees you to follow your true life-purpose. By the time you have finished this book, I hope, you will know the cause of many of your imbalances, and insecurities, and what heightens them. You will also know the steps to take to help heal yourself. If you follow them, it will take you a step closer to uncovering your true purpose.

Perhaps you cannot see it yet, but you are already following your true life-purpose. The challenges you have endured and overcome are all part of it. Even reading this book is part of your destiny; as were the steps that led you to finding it. The information, within these pages, are meant for you. Even if you are not yet ready, for the material presented, the seeds are being planted for when you are.

Finding Your Path

One of the most frustrating questions to have burning within anyone's life is: 'What is my purpose in life?' I know only too well how bothersome it is to have that question unanswered and smoldering at the back of the mind. Because they have this incredible gift, for an Empath, it is exasperating to be waiting to find their path. Few even know what purpose their gift serves and this in itself is tormenting. Sadly, until they have come to master it, most can only see being an Empath as a hindrance which holds them back from enjoying life.

I have often been asked: 'How can I be of service to others when I feel so low?' or 'I want to help but how should I do it?' It is an inbred trait for Empaths to want to help those who are suffering. To be sitting on the sidelines, watching others suffer, frustrates the Empath no-end. Some may have found, when they try to help friends or family, their help was not wanted. It is soul-destroying to see another suffering and not be able to assist them. The fact is most people do not want to hear what they could be doing to reshape their life. And it is not your job to make them 'see'. It is their journey and their responsibility. The best an Empath can do is live by example. Transform yourself and be an inspiration. When you rewrite your own script, people notice. If they see you living an empowered life they often want to know how you did it.

It is often the case that when people want to help fix others it is because they do not know where to begin in fixing their own lives. In the Empath's case, if they can't repair themselves, they want to help take another person's pain away because they know, only to well, how awful it feels.

The good thing about being an Empath is you are constantly presented with ways to transform and heal your life, you just don't always know how to recognize your own intuition's promptings. When you make the necessary changes, your intuition becomes audible and you learn how to navigate it. Unnecessary suffering then becomes a thing of the past.

Society tells us that suffering is bad. But, it is through suffering humans evolve. Through an Empath's anguish, they often look for a new and better path in life. Emotional pain also opens the door for an important rite of passage into spiritual consciousness.

Many feel like they are suffering when they do not know their purpose in life. Every Empath needs direction and purpose, no matter how evolved they are, and it is up to each of them to seek it out. When you look for answers you will always find them, it is then up to you to follow the signs.

106

To serve their life purpose, some Empaths believe they should be working closely with others. This often proves to be a testing option because of the getting "peopled" factor. But Empaths do not have to work directly with others to be of service—unless that is their purpose and passion—there are many other vocational options that do not involve much people interaction from working with animals to working creatively from home.

Within this Secret I hope to help you uncover where you purpose lies so you can spread your wings and fly.

Crazy Working Environments

For the Empath, feeling confused, whether they are on the right vocational path, is common. Even if they enjoy their work they may feel they are meant for something else. Because they get emotionally and physically exhausted, by spending too much time around others, it may create feelings of unfulfillment within their work. Low vitality may also hold them back from uncovering their intended direction.

Wearing other people's emotions and energy, like many Empaths unintentionally do, is physically and emotionally exhausting. Exhaustion makes you dispirited. So, no matter how much you enjoy your work, this crushing enervation may make you question or blame your job. An out-of-balance Empath will always become drained, if they are overstimulated with energy, which can lead to unhappiness or depression. The overstimulation does not have to stem from negative energy either. Being around too much excitement, exhilaration, nervousness or other wired emotions—whether they belong to the Empath or not—can cause burn-out. Once the Empath finds balance, in their mind, body and spirit, the exhaustion is often negated by doing a job they have a burning passion for. The next 2 secrets cover why an empath becomes physically and energetically unbalanced, as well as ways to rectify it, but for now we will look at ways to bring you face to face with your true vocation (if you are not already in it).

Spending too much time around highly charged, or negative, energy is mostly destructive for the Empath. And this is why working in places like hospitals, where there is lots of anxious energy, can lead the Empath to exhaustion and depression. Because Empaths are caring and nurturing, and have a keen desire to help those suffering, a hospital may seem like the perfect place to be of service. But if they are out-of-balance a hospital will be one of the most toxic places for them, energetically. After a lifetime of being an Empath, and the challenges that go with it, the Empath's body becomes less resilient, this becomes more evident after the age of thirty. A weak body leads to a weak mind, emotional body, and energy field. This is a major contributor to leaky aura syndrome. When you have a leaky aura, your energy leaks out and other people's energy pours in (see next Secret), which can cause anything from depression to angry outbursts. Every Empath experiences it differently, but leaky aura is never a pleasant thing to experience. Therefore, you tend to feel constantly dissatisfied and, until you find balance, it is difficult to uncover your true purpose. When your mental and physical energy is cluttered, you cannot think clearly or access your true intuition.

As a general rule, if you are deeply unhappy in your job, and dread going there each day, that job is not for you. Staying in a job you hate will weaken you in every way. Your energy will plummet, being around people is torturous, and you may constantly feel rundown or ill. Fact! This is why I cannot stress enough about finding overall balance. As an Empath, you face so many challenges and are incredibly vulnerable to the modern world. If you were to go to a doctor, he may label you as a hypochondriac and send you off with anti-depressants. Sadly, pharmaceuticals are of no help to an Empath.

It may seem strange that I am discussing finding balancing at the same time as finding your life purpose, but when your life is clouded with energy, belonging to others, finding your own heart's desire is near impossible to do.

Getting back to work, Empaths do not do well working long hours or working in stressful or overstimulating environments. But if this is an environment you have chosen, and really enjoy, you have to be extra vigilante of self-protection as well as finding ways to make the job better suit you as an Empath. For example: working shorter hours, having scheduled breaks and taking plenty of holidays. It is also advantageous to become the boss and make your own flexible working hours.

There is a perfect vocation for every Empath but it may involve stepping out of their comfort zone to get there. Most Empaths already have an idea of what they would like to try, as an inner-yearning, but they may convince themselves it is an unrealistic goal. Either because they have never tried it before or they feel too old, they may put themselves off attempting anything new because of their doubts. Doubt is an Empaths greatest traitor. Their intuition may guide them towards their destined path but their doubts often lead them away from it.

Let Your Intuition Guide You

If an Empath spends too much time around those who do not believe in themselves, esteem issues may inadvertently become part of their own life-story. As discussed in the last Secret, discovering what energy, or insecurities, belongs to whom is a major part of the Empath's re-balancing process. Unfortunately, it is not an overnight procedure. There are layers to unpeel and, just like when un-layering an onion, it may bring tears to the eyes. When looking for a new career low self-confidence often holds the, out-of-balance, Empath back. I say out-of-balance because balanced Empaths do not have esteem issues. Their inner-power overcomes any concerns of self-doubt. Accessing and utilizing your intuition is one of the best ways to find clues about your perfect profession. Your inner-Knowing has more clout than you may realize. You often just need to ask the right questions.

I don't believe an Empath's intuition is ever wrong. Most just don't listen to it or know how to interpret its signs. As part of an important life lesson, your intuition may push you into a place of suffering, and because of this you stop trusting it. As already mentioned, suffering is not always bad. You can learn more from failure and hard times than you ever could from the good.

111

Experiencing tough times may also be preparation for your new journey.

Empaths came here to learn and evolve. This is another reason why you always feel like you are searching. Your active imaginations drive you towards finding new information and wisdom, even new jobs.

Some Empaths may find themselves going from job to job, learning new skills and trades. Believing they are searching for a job that fits. But there may be another reason... You could be multipotentialite Empath!

What is a Multipotentialite?

According to Emilie Wapnick: A multipotentialite is a person who has many different interests and creative pursuits in life. She says:

'Multipotentialites have no "one true calling" the way specialists do. Being a multipotentialite is our destiny. We have many paths and we pursue all of them, either sequentially or simultaneously (or both).

Multipotentialites thrive on learning, exploring, and mastering new skills. We are excellent at bringing disparate ideas together in creative ways. This makes us incredible innovators and problem solvers.

When it comes to new interests that emerge, our insatiable curiosity leads us to absorb everything we can get our hands on. As a result, we pick up new skills fast and tend to be a wealth of information.'

Many Empaths resonate with being a multipotentialite for the simple fact they love to learn and master new skills.

Becoming skilled in several professions is normal for an Empath. They are good at most things they are drawn to, but they will not fare well in tasks or trades forced upon them. If a multipotentialite Empath child is made to do schoolwork they find boring, or pointless, they will not excel at it. Empath children often find subjects, presented by the education system, meaningless and are un-engaged by them. And thus, will not fare well in their studies. I mention this because if you are a multipotentialite at heart, and did not do well at school, you may carry a fear of trying anything new. If you were not sufficiently engaged by the choice of work given to you, as a child, you will not have excelled at it. You may have then grown up believing you have no talent for anything and thus a fear of trying anything new.

As a child, I did not enjoy school, there was very little about it that pressed my buttons. This was not because I did not want to learn, I love learning and gaining knowledge, but I did not want to learn about what I considered to be unnecessary to life. I often got into trouble with teachers. They thought I was not trying when really, I was just not interested. As an adult, I know my Empath intuition was always guiding me, even when my school teachers weren't.

We live in a society where one is expected to choose and stay on one vocational path for life which is often pre-determined in childhood. This in itself is ridiculous. People go through massive transitions every ten years or so. What was a fit in someone's twenties is not a fit in their forties. Jobs included. That said, for some, being in the same job throughout life is "heaven on a plate", but this path is not for everyone. Some need to keep changing, keep learning, and keep moving forward.

Because an Empath feels the judgments of others, it may hold them back from attempting any new career. They may not want to be judged for being flaky or inconsistent or they may fear failure. If you want to walk a new path, you have to take fear out of the equation. It only holds you back. When you face fear, and step out of your comfort zone, you grow exponentially, fact! It also puts you on track to finding your bliss.

Do not worry about trying new things and it not working out, or you deciding you don't want to do it as a career. Whatever you learn it will always takes you somewhere new.

Like many others, I believed I studied different subjects, and professions, because I was looking for my "one true calling". But, like you, I've always been on the right path. What I learnt, or experienced, at different stages in my life, was all part of my journey and life purpose. They were stepping stones to a bigger picture. What I've studied, over the years, has been for more than the reason of indulging a passion and healing myself. Everything I know now, about healing the Empath, has come from what I learnt. But when I started my research, twenty years ago, I had no idea I would end up writing about the subject for others. I now love writing about ways others can better serve themselves and uncovering all I have has helped me do this.

All Empaths have the potential to find their inner-greatness and walk an empowered path. Knowledge is a force that helps them harness and unleash their hidden power. There is nothing wrong with embracing change, having a desire to learn or a thirst for knowledge. Stepping away from the fearful masses, and herd mentality, is essential for growth. You have to know it is ok to keep learning and experiencing new or different careers; if that is what you want.

You can create any life you desire. The world is your oyster. If you have an inner-calling, follow it. It is your life and your call. Live how you want to live! The great late Wayne Dyer used to say: *'Don't die with your music still inside you!'* This saying is a reminder to keep following, and listening to, your intuition. If you have a hankering to follow a certain path do it… Oh and don't wait!

No one can never be sure when their number is up. Life shouldn't be wasted believing you can't or shouldn't. If it feels right, then it is right. Don't wait until you're sixty to do what you wanted to try in your forties. And don't be afraid of trying too many things. You never know where what you learnt today will take you tomorrow.

Finding Your Vocation

You may now be thinking that you have no idea of what you could try as a new career. You may know you want to try a new path, or many new paths, but don't know how or where to start. So, let's take look at ways in which you can better find your dream vocation.

I have adapted the following exercises from the book 'Success Principles' by Jack Canfield. They are designed to give you a point of reference and act as a guide to which direction you could be going in life. The exercises are not just ways to find one vocation but to get you thinking towards what direction you could go in life.

It is a series of questions aimed at your unconscious mind. Repeatedly questioning your subconscious accesses your intuition and is one of the best ways to get to your truth. I find the exercises works best when your mind is calm and quiet. Doing a ten-minute meditation, or some breathing exercise (see tools section), beforehand will allow access to your subconscious and still your ego mind. (If you give your ego a voice it will probably tell you the only way to happiness is by getting rich, famous, and influential.)

Before you sit to meditate make sure you have some paper and a pen (or your dream journal for manifestation - more on that shortly) on hand. Focus on a question such as: 'show me my path.' When you open your eyes, answer the following questions, by writing them down quickly and honestly.

Take the Quiz

1. What are your passions?
2. What do you love to learn and read up on?
3. What do you believe would make everyone happier?
4. What would you wake up excited to do each day?
5. What job would you do for free?
6. What can you not live without doing?
7. What engages you?
8. What interest keeps coming back to you?
9. What would your perfect conversation be about?
10. If you could change the world for the better, how would you do it?

How Did You Do?

The above exercise can be done as many times as you wish. It is good to try both exercises several times to see if your answers match up.

Now onto the next exercise. The following questions are designed to get you thinking a little harder and deeper and will hopefully make you aware of where your path lies. Answer the questions as fast as you can:

Quiz Number Two

1. What do you consider to be your best qualities

2. Write down two ways you like to use these qualities when connecting with others…

3. If the world was a perfect place how would it look to you? How is everyone interacting with you and each other…?

4. Combine the above three answers and reword them into a single statement paragraph, adding in what feels intuitively right…

If you tried the above exercises more than once and the answers stayed mostly the same your path is being shown. If they differ or contradict each other, you may have multiple paths or are not quite ready for you new direction. Did any of the answers match up with the answers you gave on the last exercise? You will, at the least, see a pattern in your desires for life. I would hazard a guess that the theme of your answers revolves around helping others. Do not be put off by this if you get wiped-out by being around people. When you've read this book in its entirety you will understand why Empaths experience all they do. And if you follow the advice given in this book, right up to the last page, you will be amazed at how your life can transform. Your energy levels will rise, your happiness will skyrocket and it will become obvious which direction you should be going. The changes you experience can be felt and have a knock-on-effect on those around you. You will willingly spend longer periods of time around others, or happily spend time alone, and joyfulness becomes a staple in your life.

Once you have determined what your purpose in life is keep looking at ways to fulfil it. Remember, it may not be doing just one thing. You may have multiple jobs or pastimes ahead.

Follow Your Calling

Everything that shows up in your life has reason and that includes urges to try certain vocations. You may have an urge to learn photography or try your hand at being an astrologer. But gave yourself a reason not to try it. Empaths are good at talking themselves out of doing things, especially if they involve stepping out of their comfort zone. Don't listen to your irrational doubts and instead follow your intuition.

There is hidden potential in every opportunity even if you cannot see it at the time. Everything that shows up in your life is the universe trying to put you on the right path. The universe cannot force you into taking action, only you can do that. If you make the first move, the universe will then meet you half-way and help you build a new path. But nothing will happen until you first take action!

For the Empath, finding their calling or vocation may seem like an arduous task. But living a lie, through having to pretend you like a job you detest, or sell a product you have no faith in, only leads to more unhappiness. Being unhappy in work is no way to spend your precious short life. Time moves quickly. Before you know it, you will be at the end of this earthly visit. Those years you could have spent indulging your passions, exploring or learning new ways or being, are wasted. Eighty percent of the global workforce do not enjoy their chosen vocation. Now is your chance to become part of the twenty percent thriving in their work.

Passive Income

It is wise to think ahead when delving into a new career for the simple reason it may not happen overnight. Although it may be the root of all evil, you still need money to survive. Whatever path you chose, you have to pay the bills and keep a roof over your head. If you want to leave your job, or start a new journey, making sure you have an income to live off, during the transition period, is important. Setting up a passive income is a great way to do this. A passive income is where you receive a guaranteed monthly income without having to put the working hours in every day. There are numerous ways to do this but a good internet search is one of the best way of getting suitable ideas. Here is a small compilation of some of my own ideas. If you have writing skills, why not release books on Amazon's Kindle? It is not always guaranteed, but by publishing your own work could generate a small, or big, monthly income. If you have money to invest in property, you can collect a monthly income from rental. Why not rent out your own property and become a lodger or house sitter? You could invest in a small holiday home rental or boat hire. Rent out your garage or even a parking space on your driveway.

If you know you have money coming in each month, to pay the bills and for food, you then have the opportunity to study or train in your chosen new profession.

Dream Journal for Manifestation

A good place to manifest your dream life is in a journal. Before you materialize anything, you need to know what you want. This is where your journal comes in. At the start of your journal write what it is you want to do or achieve in life. Think big and follow your passions. Envisioning your perfect life is part of creating it. Picture it in your head as if it were happening today and write down what you see. Here's a few examples: Having the mortgage paid off and a disposable income which gives you the freedom to work part time. To be working in a dream job whilst enjoying lots of free time to travel abroad. Owning a cottage in the country with a special garden room where you can spend hours writing.

Next, write down what you intend to do this year to start the ball rolling. For example: downsize the current house to help pay off the mortgage, take a course at college or online, or gain experience by offering to work voluntary.

Now, break it down even further. How do you intend to do each one? For example: Get a house valuation done and find out how to maximize the sale price. Research, or enrol on, college courses or explore ways of setting up your own business. Look at places where you may like to work.

On a daily, or weekly, basis write down what you have done to make your ambition come to fruition. How many steps closer are you to its realization? You will be amazed how fast you see things manifest once you set your intention and follow the steps towards your aspirations. It does not matter if you do not know what job you would like to do at this time. Just write down your vision of how you would like your life to be. Your Dream Journal of Manifestation is not set in stone. It can change and have new dreams added to it or taken away. Just make sure, no matter how small, you do something each week to manifest them. Don't wait for someone else to do it for you or expect it to land on your lap. That won't happen. Take over the reins of your life today. Do not fear failure. There is no such thing. Everything is experience. And don't allow the judgments of others to hold you back. It does not matter what others think. Let others use their ideas, and judgements, to shape their life, not yours.

When you depart this body you only get to take with you your experiences. Make as many of them as you can. Life is about experiences. Only society expects you to stay in one job for the rest of your days. Remember you are the architect of your own reality and your dreams can become an actuality!

Don't Let Fear Hold You Back

Taking any kind of risk is scary. When you take risks, you are not given a guarantee of success. The only guarantee you have is the belief in yourself. Whatever you believe you will prove yourself right.

Hoping something will work out is not enough. You have to truly believe. Fear of failure will stop you moving forward, fact! You have to stay constant in your belief of yourself. And this is where your Dream Journal for Manifestation comes in again.

Your journal is not just to put down your dreams and intentions. It is a place where you can give yourself pep-talks and calm your worries. Within your journal, you become your own cheerleader! By writing down your fears, it is a great way to resolve them. When you face your fears, by addressing them on paper, you access your intuition. By regularly unburdening yourself, in your journal, the answers to obstacles, you may encounter, come almost magically. Truthfully expressing your woes, through the written word, is unbelievably cathartic and also beneficial for your soul growth.

Whatever you write in your journal always finish on a positive note. Ending on a positive note keeps you in the right mental space to continue manifesting your goals. It also ensures your journal stays supportive and encouraging. All of which are the perfect dream-generating conditions! Never give up on any of your aspirations. Perseverance is all you need. Keep working. Take small steps each day, week, month and year, and see your life transform. You have already created what you have in your life now. You created it because you believed you could. Take this belief and use it to manifest your ideal life!

Feel Gratitude

Regularly expressing gratitude sends a message to the universe and the universe responds by giving you more to be grateful for. If you make it a daily practice your energy signature changes and your body, mind and spirit work will together to seek out new ways to be grateful.

Staying in the present moment also helps. If you only focus on your destination you miss the present and all the magical moments it offers. Being grateful for every experience along the way, both good and bad, not only makes life more enjoyable but makes you happier as an Empath.

I have learnt more from having bad experiences than I have from the good. There have been some incredibly trying times in my life. Times where one thing after another would build up and bring me down. But a change in my attitude was all it took to get me through those challenges. I started to believe that everything would work out, no matter how bad a situation got. I told myself everything is, and was, in divine order. I learnt it was my thoughts that made a situation unbearable and not the situation itself. I then found it easier to express gratitude for every experience.

Being grateful for bad experiences is no easy task when going through tough times but believing everything is, or will be, okay, and being grateful for that, is doable. When you come through the other side of any dark or challenging times, you can always find an amazing lesson hidden within its shadows. When you look for the good in everything you will find it.

Dark Times

Dark times are a natural passage of life. You do not get to choose them but they will happen. Some Empaths, however, find they spend more time in a dark place than in a light one. If this applies to you, you may be ignoring your intuition's promptings for you to make changes.

Your intuition is your guide and wayshower. It will constantly point you towards the changes you need to make. If you ignore it, the signals get louder and more painful.

All humans try to avoid pain. But pain can be an incredible catalyst for making change. Darkness, depression and unhappiness are signs of imbalance. But because so many people experience depression, or low-moods, it has become accepted as a normal way of being. It is not! You are supposed to be happy and enjoying life!

The biggest changes, and transformations, happen for any human when they make adjustments to rebalance their mind, body and spirit. When you become balanced depression, mood

128

swings and apathy become a thing of the past. Please do not think eternal darkness is part of an Empath's destiny. It's not! It is just a sign of imbalance.

By the time you have read the next two secrets, you will be armed with all the information needed to start your Empath transformation. Your intuition has already been nudging about the changes you need to make and now is the time to listen. As I already mentioned, it is not by accident that you are reading this book, but knowledge alone is not enough. Transformation requires you to make changes.

Ask yourself how you can improve this day. How you can improve yourself? How can you make someone else's life a little better by what you do? And how can you strive towards achieving your goal? Write it down and see what your answers are.

When you strive to get better in life, life will get better. At the gym, work a little harder, when at work try to be a little nicer to others, improve your diet, learn something new each day and rise above limiting beliefs! Be grateful now for all the miraculous changes coming your way and it will serve in speeding up the process!

If there is one thing that will stop you from achieving your dreams it is unconstructive self-talk. Empaths dislike to listen to others, who talk negatively, so they should not stand for it from themselves. You have a choice about what or who you listen to. You are not helping anyone by allowing yourself, or others, to indulge in self-defeating talk. Trying to remain in a positive, happy place is the way forward. Being happy will attract more reasons to be happy.

When you are positive your brain is 31% more productive than when stressed or negative. It also raises your intelligence, creativity and energy. Being exposed to negativity brings the Empath down faster than anything and will stop them manifesting their true desires.

Once you change your energy signature, by taking the steps laid out in this book, you will find you attract more and more reasons to be cheerful, along with more people who make you cheerful. Anyone of a negative nature will no longer enjoy being in your presence because you vibrate too high for them. You no longer need to avoid them because they avoid you.

The best way to find your wings and your true purpose is by firstly finding and healing yourself as an Empath. The past two secrets were written to help you find yourself and the next two will help you heal. So, without further ado let's move to the next Secret...

Secret 6

What Breaks the Empath?

Life as an Empath is a brilliant, remarkable voyage and a fast-paced rollercoaster ride. That is not to say Empath life is easy, it really isn't. But if it was, you would not get the amazing sense of accomplishment from overcoming the many difficulties you have. An Empath can climb mountains, float on a cloud and stumble into darkness; sometimes all in one day. You may not see it at the time, but the experiences you face always lead to self-advancement. Empath challenges pave the way for evolvement. And, finding new ways to become better is always going to be rewarding!

As an Empath, I have, by no means, got all the answers to life. Nor would I yet want to. Life is about learning and we have to leave something to discover on life's path. However, the most important detail I have learnt to date is the Empath will never find complete stability until they have balance in their mind, body and spirit.

The mind is the thoughts, ego and emotions. The body is the physical vessel. And the spirit is the invisible self; comprising of the soul, aura and energy centers (chakras and meridians).

Every Empath is different. Each exceptional in their own mind, body and spirit and, when it comes to re-balancing, what works for one does not always work for another.

Being an individual, you need to discover for yourselves what works to heal and balance yourself; through trial and error. Some Empaths need speeding up, some need slowing down, some will benefit from a high protein diet, some a high-carbohydrate diet, some need to get out of their heads and some need to get inside their heads. Because of individuality, the path for you to connect your mind, body and spirit is unique to you. However, there are some specific steps that apply to all.

Trinity Healing

All humans come as a trinity package of mind, body and spirit. For complete balance, all three need to be in unison. Some need to balance all three, others need only work on one area to be healed in total. For example: one person may have emotional scars, brought forward from previous lives, which are healed through past-life regression (spirit). Another may find blocked chakras, caused by a childhood trauma, dissolved after a series of crystal therapy sessions (spirit or mind). One may have a busy, or angry, mind cured by a daily meditation practice (mind) and for another a regular yoga practice may calm the nervous system, healing a stress-related illness (body).

When it comes to Empath re-balancing it is never a straight forward process. Because they are sensitive and endure powerful emotions, through the law of attraction they drawn in more of the same from others. It often proves a challenge, for the Empath, to stay detached from the emotional energy of the populace, especially if they have a leaky aura.

A leaky aura is one of the major contributors to Empath imbalance. Every human has an aura, or energy field, that emanates around them like a luminous egg-shaped sheath. It

135

extends around and away from the body for anything up to five feet (in a healthy person). The vibration of this energetic body is fine and subtle.

Empaths are known to have weak auras, and is one of the reasons they take on so much emotional energy, and this plays a huge role in preventing them from finding balance.

Your aura both surrounds and penetrates your body. It has seven layers corresponding with your seven main energy centers, or chakras. Information is stored within your aura. This information is an accumulation of happy and sad experiences, ideas and opinions, unreleased emotions, negative thought-forms, past life memories and toxins, etc. Because Empaths pick up energy from those they connect with, they also carry, within their aura, the thought-forms and energy belonging to others.

The Empath who is unhealthy, in their body and mind, will have a receded aura. When the aura shrinks, it weakens and often becomes permeable (energy leaks out and in). A permeable aura is also known as a leaky aura.

A leaky aura creates a merging, or clash, of energies between those in close proximity. To the Empath, this feels like an energetic parasite has attached itself and often leads to overwhelm. This integration generates too much emotional energy and often leads to Empath overwhelm.

When the aura is leaky it is bad news on many levels. Leaky aura not only allows your energy out (causing fatigue and other imbalances) but admits other's energy in, causing a frantic energy mix. Also, if an Empath comes into close proximity with anyone who themselves have a leaky aura, whether theirs is leaky or not, they soak up their energy like a super-absorbent sponge.

An impaired body and mind weakens the aura. Low-level thoughts and emotions, unbalanced chakras, food intolerances, poor diet, drugs and alcohol all impair the body, and anything that impairs the body damages the energy field and results in a leaky aura. If you are unhealthy, eat an unsuitable diet, take drugs or stimulants, drink alcohol, smoke cigarettes, experience stress and have dark thoughts you will, in all likelihood, have a leaky aura. This means the emotions and energy of others becomes etched within your energy-field.

By finding total balance of mind, body and spirit, it works something like an "energetic anti-histamine" for the Empath. A healthy body and mind results in a powerful aura and creates the

Empath's invisible armour. A formidable aura empowers the Empath. It persuades other people's energy to bounce off and is conducive for a happier life. You cannot expect your mind and spirit to be strong when you are putting something into the body that weakens it.

So, how do you repair a leaky aura? One of the easiest steps is to eliminate all drugs and drug-like foods.

An Empath's sensitivity and heightened emotions affect their brain chemistry and hormones (see next Secret). Any one hormone being out-of-sync has a knock-on-effect on all the other hormone-producing glands. Certain foods have been scientifically proven to have a drug-like effect on the human brain. This effect can then disrupt the hormones natural cycle, which then affects the chakras and the aura. Because of their Sensitivity, the Empath is already vulnerable to experiencing hormonal imbalance and for this reason it is essential they address their diet.

I used to believe I would find complete balance by becoming more "spiritual" or energetically clean. I was not aware, as I sat in meditation and performed yoga each day, that if I was putting poison into my body no amount of spiritual practice would balance me. Back then the only poison I believed was consuming was alcohol. How wrong I was. I was inadvertently consuming drug-like foods without knowing what impact they were having on my mind, body and Empath ways. The worst offender being a food that it is a staple in the Western diet and often hailed as a health food. The most profound, and beneficial, changes happened for me when I eliminated this one drug-like food: wheat!

The Grain Secretly Poisoning You

You would have to live deep underground to not have heard about the amazing transformations people are having after eliminating wheat (and not just Sensitive folk). Weight-loss, reversal of physical and mental ailments to name a few. It is shameful it has taken so long for it to come to light just how bad wheat is. But, being a multi-billion-pound industry, it is hardly surprising that they do not want the truth to come out about the damage wheat causes. Because this damage is often gradual, most do not link their physical or mental health problems with their wheat consumption. And being so addictive, means the majority of people do not want to believe how destructive wheat is to their health.

Just think about how much wheat the average person consumes: toast for breakfast, a sandwich for lunch, pizza or pasta for dinner, and that's not to mention the wheat in beer, snacks, sauces and meat, or vegetarian protein, coatings. At least 50 to 75% of, some people's, diet is made up of wheat containing foods.

If you are one of the many who believe wheat cannot be all bad, because it has been around for centuries and is a staple in the Western diet, you are not aware of this fact: wheat is not what it used to be. Wheat has been genetically altered, by scientists, to make it more resilient to weather and bugs. These changes have made it destructive to health. Since the mid-eighties, most of the Western world has been eating a hybridized version of the wheat crop. This also coincides with the rise in obesity, depression and diabetes epidemics.

Although wheat is hailed as a health food, it acts like a drug and has been scientifically proven to have a drug-like effect on the brain. Wheat has been linked with many mental and physical illnesses. It is a low-vibrational food that weakens every human, especially the Empath.

When wheat was genetically altered, its protein structure was changed. Now, when digested, wheat breaks down into many small proteins that can cross the blood-brain barrier. These tiny proteins attach themselves to the opiate receptors of the brain. This has the effect of a narcotic, but without the pleasurable high. It has been scientifically proven to encourage overeating and trigger, or worsen, mental illnesses. For the Empath, it heightens their addictive personality, their emotional state and impacts their already unbalanced brain chemistry.

Mind-Altering Food

Wheat has the power to alter your perception and natural instincts. Not only affecting how much you eat, but what you eat. It also switches off your dietary intuition designed to prevent you from choosing foods and substances damaging to your health.

If you include it in your diet, then wheat is controlling you more than you could ever know, and not just in your dietary choices. It may play a part in other addictive behaviors and is linked to controlling moods. Until you take it out of your diet, completely, then and only then will you see how it ruled your mind, moods and weight.

Empaths respond more disagreeably to drug-like foods, such as wheat, because they are highly reactive. High reactive people are extremely responsive to different vibrations of energy. They taste the bitterness in lemons more, feel emotional and physical pain more, blush easier than most and are affected by drugs and alcohol worse than those who are not highly reactive.

Everything is energy vibrating at different frequencies and that includes food, drugs or alcohol. The faster a person vibrates, the higher their frequency. Empaths are negatively affected by anything of a low vibration. Most drugs and alcohol have a low vibrational energy and will bring the Empath down fast. Wheat is not classed as a drug, but very much acts like one. Therefore, it carries the same energy signature.

People are all affected in different ways by modern wheat. It may, for example, cause digestive problems for one person, mental-health problems in another, and joint pain for another. If you suffer with unexplained physical or emotional issues, check your diet. Low moods, lethargy, digestive issues, depression and more are linked to wheat. You may not eat bread but you could still consume lots of wheat. It is hidden in many foods for the reason it keeps people consuming more of it.

Drug-Like Action of Wheat

When I explain to others the remarkable changes that happened in my life, just by eliminating wheat, I see their eyes glaze over. I feel them go within themselves. I understand they do not want to hear the benefits of wheat elimination because they do not want to give it up. They do not comprehend that being a drug, they are addicted to wheat and it is actually their addiction creating the resistance. If I told them eliminating apples would turn their life around, most wouldn't think twice about ditching them... because apples aren't addictive.

Many Empaths believe their emotional welfare is only compromised by absorbing too much negative energy. And although several Empath miseries are indeed caused by the above, they will be worsened by what they consume. I found much of my emotional "Empath stuff" was caused by wheat proteins. I appreciate not everyone will have the same life-changing benefits I did, or the thousands of others who have also eliminated wheat. But by wheat's elimination, your Empath life, and overall general health, will very likely turn around.

Humans are ready to evolve and raise their vibration. Evolving means uniting mind, body and spirit. This can only be done by removing anything of a low vibration from one's life. This means eliminating anything that affects the smooth running of the brain and body. When anything low vibrational, which alters the mood and perception, is eliminated you see amazing changes in your life, fact! Doing so plugs you back into your innate intuition. This clears your vision and allows your true path to be revealed.

Giving up wheat was the catalyst for a total life-transformation for me. When I removed this single grain from my diet, I removed a drug I did not know I was consuming. I then saw how other foods affected my health and Empath wellbeing. Within a year of removing wheat I had completely changed my diet and stopped drinking alcohol. I am happier and more confident than I have ever been in my entire adult life.

When you remove wheat from your diet you can then see just how much it controlled your moods, appetite and mind. It will also allow you to see what other changes need to be made. By removing drug-like foods from your life it gives your intuition a voice. Your body may take a while to heal from a lifetime's consumption of wheat. But the good news is your mind heals very quickly and your intuition kicks up several notches.

If you do it, make sure you eliminate wheat 100%. Reducing your intake by 75% or even 80% will not see the changes you want. You may feel better for a while, but the addiction will still be there. The amount of wheat you eat will creep back up and, before you know it, you are eating the same amount you were, if not more. This also reinforces your addiction to wheat. Your mind will then do anything to stop you from giving up wheat again. Eliminate wheat 100% for four weeks and see for yourself the amazing changes.

By changing your diet and tuning into your body's needs, it allows your true Self to emerge. Foods that act like drugs cause all humans damage. To the Empaths, who already have hormone and chemical imbalances, drug-like foods are destructive. Wheat is not the only drug-like food that Empaths should avoid, the other is refined sugar.

Refined Sugar and the Empath

As you will be aware, white sugar has no nutritional value. It is a toxic sweetener linked with diabetes, premature aging, obesity and many other diseases. Having a similar effect on the brain as wheat, white sugar acts as an opiate and triggers physical and mental disorders.

145

The sole purpose of food is to provide the body with nourishment and fuel to stay alive. As refined sugar has no nutrients, it has no benefit being included in the diet. Refined sugar is worse for the body and mind than cocaine, and more addictive, yet it is in most processed foods. Just like wheat, when you've kicked the habit and got sugar out of the system, the desire is gone for good. Have a small amount of it, however, and you will be back where you started.

White sugar is inflammatory. If you have any health problems refined sugar will make them worse. Just because your body may look healthy on the outside does not mean there are no troubles within. Removing sugar from your diet acts as a safeguard against illness.

Wheat and refined sugar rob the body of essential nutrients and enzymes. An imbalance of just one nutrient, or enzyme, can cause illness and depression, it can plunge you into the depths of despair, cause chronic fatigue and sleepless nights. It will also lead to a low-quality of life.

Without enzymes, you would cease to exist. They keep you alive, nourish your bodies and keep your mind healthy. As you age, your enzyme production decreases. This, coupled with a bad diet, puts you on a fast-tracked-path to mental and physical illness. As an Empath, this is more reason to keep your enzyme consumption high and eliminate foods, such as wheat and sugar, that deplete them.

Enzymes are found in all fruits and vegetables; but are especially abundant when the food is in its raw state. They can also be purchased in supplement form.

Giving up much loved foods, such as wheat and sugar, is not a simple task, I know. Your mind will fight to keep them in your diet. However, once out of the system, those cravings subside and you will not miss them. You will be amazed at just how fantastic you feel. For those who have suffered a lifelong battle with ailments, allergies, fatigue and illness, you will be astounded at just how much these foods affected you.

When you give up any drug-like food, or drink, your body will go through withdrawal symptoms; normally lasting from a few days up to a few weeks. I have listed some of the symptoms you can expect to endure, during elimination, in the Tools section. I have also listed ways in which to cope with them.

Modern diets and lifestyles have taken too many people down without them realizing. Because the Empaths are already vulnerable to anything that lowers their vibration, it is essential all foods that have a drug-like effect, on the body and mind, are eliminated. If you suffer with trauma triggers or any type of emotional or stress disorder you will also benefit from their elimination, because consuming wheat, or sugar, worsen their control.

If you want to heal yourself and discover what your true role in life is, eliminate any artificial, genetically modified or hybridized foods. The root cause of many problems in both body and mind is what you feed on. An inappropriate diet can literally turn you into a sleepwalker; incapable of thinking for yourself. Until you clean up your diet, and give your body what it needs to thrive, you will likely not find your true purpose or reach anything close to the enlightened state you may aspire for.

Because of Sensitivity stress, and what they take on from others, when it comes to health and wellbeing, Empaths are already at a disadvantage. They have to work harder than most to stay in balance and they need to be extra vigilante with their diet. Too often, the debilitating feelings many experience (Sensitive or not), mentally and physically, are blamed on stress at home or work, past traumas, external energies or being peopled. But believe me, they are not **all** caused by that. If the hectic emotions, an Empath suffers with, are not caused directly by drug-like foods, they are most definitely worsened by them.

Only when you clean up your diet will you understand just how much the wrong diet hinders your Empath health, spiritual progress and happiness.

So far, I have explained two toxic substances for an Empath, wheat and refined sugar, the third is alcohol. Although most drink alcohol as a way to relax or as a way to have fun it often has the opposite effect. It may seem that alcohol gives you confidence, it doesn't, it makes you more fearful and holds you back from your true potential.

It is not my intention to be a killjoy, but these three indulgences, wheat, refined sugar and alcohol, suppress you and your abilities more than you could imagine. They keep you enslaved and in fear. You only come to discover how destructive they are when you eliminate them.

Sensitive people do not do well on any drug-like food or drink, and whilst consuming them they will not excel in life. I write this from experience. I used to consume all three and I cannot tell you how much my life has transformed since eliminating them. Any kind of stimulant will only serve in weakening the Empath; as they do any other human.

Alcohol, Why It Holds You Back!

Many Empaths use alcohol and drugs to block out other people's emotions, especially at social events. I can categorically state it does not and will never work! Under the influence, it may feel like the emotions off others are being blocked but this is not the case. Alcohol does not block other people's energy, if anything, it enhances its effect and will leave you filled with fear and ill-feelings for days after. How do I know? I drank for thirty years of my life. Now I no longer imbibe, I can see exactly what effect it had on Empath life!

Most, but not all, Empaths are introvert in nature. Introverts dislike small talk, they need their conversations to have depth and meaning. They do not fare well in the social environments the rest of the extrovert world thrives on. Busy social settings are hard-work for the Empath, making them feel drained or overworked. Because the social traits of an introvert Empath are not seen as acceptable, in this extrovert world, many turn to alcohol to help them cope in social situations. They hope the alcohol will aid their conversations and make them more relaxed. But, in the long term, alcohol does not make the Empath happy. To be happy, an Empath needs to be authentic and true to themselves. Alcohol prevents this from happening.

If alcohol is used to help in social events, the Empath will become dependent on it. They then believe they cannot have a good time without it. When you become aware of being an Empath, you come to realize, if you drink alcohol, you often do so to handle being in certain people's presence for any length of time. You may also believe alcohol blocks out other people's emotions and numbs pain. It really doesn't!

When I was younger, I had fun times whilst drinking at parties. Back then I liked the social scene. But the more alcohol I drank the weaker and more fearful I became (although I had no idea of this at the time). The older I got, the more my introvert Empath traits kicked in and the less I enjoyed the party lifestyle. After the age of twenty-five my main reason for drinking, I thought, was to give me the ability to be around people comfortably. It also helped me engage with those I had nothing in common with. I assumed it lowered my "negative energy sensors". But alcohol just slowed down my reactions to it. I still had to deal with the energy I acquired off others, but I had to deal with it at the same time as my physical hangover.

I did not understand that, being an introvert Empath, I would never enjoy being around large groups of people. But no one had taught me this. I thought I was shy and believed alcohol gave me more confidence. It didn't. It was quite the opposite. Alcohol just made me feel bad all the time. In reality, the only thing alcohol brought to my life was fear, fear and more fear. I feared being judged, I feared not fitting in and I feared people not liking me for who I really was. These are all normal fears, and a natural part of social and tribal acceptance. The problem was these fears were heightened tenfold by alcohol. I could not find my true-self, not because of all the Empath stuff I had to deal with but because alcohol, combined with wheat consumption, was holding me back.

Drinking alcohol will not bring you peace of mind. It is not a release valve, and it does not help you relax after a long day at work. These are just illusions and what we tell ourselves to justify our drinking habits.

Alcohol makes you ill, overweight, anxious, scared and fearful. It heightens any negative emotions, whether your own or those picked up off others. Alcohol holds you back from taking risks in life or stepping from your comfort zone. If you reach for alcohol every time you feel uncomfortable, it blocks any chance for growth or self-development.

The reason I gave up alcohol was because I was fed up of feeling rubbish all the time. By giving up wheat I could see how damaging alcohol was. I knew it was not making me happy... far from it. I listened to my intuition, which for too long I had ignored; telling me it was okay to give up alcohol. I had no idea how fearful alcohol was making me or how much it held me back. Until I gave it up.

My life has now transformed. I have never felt this contented in my adult life. Alcohol suppresses parts of the brain responsible for joy and happiness. People drink alcohol to have fun but, the irony is, alcohol takes away the ability to have natural fun.

Like attracts like! If you are fearful and drink alcohol guess what you feel more of? More fear! Even drinking just two glasses of wine a week is enough to keep you in a state of distress. Giving up the booze does not have to be difficult. It is as simple as deciding you want to transform your life and reach your true potential. You may have to give up your social life for a while. Four weeks is normally all it takes to get the drug out of your body. But believe me, it is so worth it.

As a side-note, if you do decide to give up alcohol be prepared to face a backlash. Others will detest the fact you are kicking a habit they are dependent on and will often try to talk you out of it. It is your life and you cannot and should not drink to please others. In the UK, especially, alcohol is the only drug you have to justify not taking.

Giving up wheat, refined sugar and alcohol will transform your life and health, fact! It is difficult to find lasting happiness unless you are healthy. You will never have a healthy body, or mind, if you eat drug-like foods. This is why, as an Empath, it is essential to address your diet.

Caffeine is another drug you may eventually decide to remove from your life, but we will get to that in the next Secret. Now, whilst we are on the subject of how your diet affects your health and wellbeing, I would just like to cover the subject of autoimmune disease:

The Empath and Autoimmune Disease

Autoimmunity is becoming a 21st century curse with more and more people being diagnosed. In America alone it is said there are at least 50 million people suffering with autoimmune disease. Anyone and everyone is at risk, but those with a genetic predisposition are a third more likely to develop one. There are varying factors in developing autoimmune disease but one of the known triggers is stress and emotional overload. It is this factor which makes the Empath more at risk.

Autoimmune disease is caused by the immune system losing the ability to differentiate between proteins belonging to your own body (like the organs, glands and muscles) and proteins belonging to a foreign invader such as bacteria, viruses and parasites. One of the most commonly known autoimmune diseases is Celiac, an extreme intolerance to gluten. If someone with Celiac consumes gluten the immune system attacks not only the gluten proteins, in the body, but the intestinal wall. This leads to excessive stomach pain, chronic diarrhea or constipation, an inability to absorb essential nutrients and many other problems. However, not all autoimmune diseases are that obvious.

Having fatigue, exhaustion, cold hands and feet, joint pain, weight problems, sore throat, eczema, psoriasis, headaches, any bowel complaint, mental disorders, low moods and depression can all be caused by autoimmune disease. To see if you are at risk of having autoimmune disease see the following questions.

If you answer yes to one or more of these questions you are higher risk. These questions include common symptoms of several autoimmune diseases:

- Did you have asthma or allergies as a child?
- Have you ever had acne, dermatitis, eczema or psoriasis?
- Have you suffered with digestive disturbances: IBS, constipation, Crohns or Celiac?
- Do you experience chronic fatigue?
- Have you got hormonal imbalances?
- Have you been diagnosed with Diabetes?
- Have you been diagnosed with a thyroid disorder?
- Do you have weight problems?
- Are you excessively introvert?
- Do you have joint, muscle or back problems?
- Do you suffer headaches?
- Do you have hay fever?
- Do you have arthritis or arthritic pain?
- Do you have high cholesterol?
- Do you get excessively hot or cold?
- Do you have white spots or patches on your skin?
- Do you suffer thinning hair?

- Do you struggle to sleep at night even though you are tired?
- Do you suffer low moods, depression or find your mood fluctuates?

One problem when trying to identify autoimmune disorders is they are difficult to diagnose (it can take years to get an accurate diagnosis by a medical practitioner). The symptoms are similar from one autoimmune disease to another. But if you have one, you are more at risk from low energy, depression, brain fog and emotional overwhelm.

Generally, wherever there is an autoimmune disease there will also be leaky gut syndrome. This means there is an increase in permeability of the intestinal lining and large gaps form between the cells of the colon. These gaps allow undigested food particles, proteins, toxins and bacteria into the bloodstream. When this material gets into the bloodstream the immune system kicks in to get it out and this can be the start of an autoimmune disease.

Hippocrates, the father of medicine, is known to have said: *all disease begins in the gut.* This is proving to be accurate.

What Causes Leaky Gut?

There are many causes of a permeable intestinal lining. The most common being: **stress**, medications, Candida, alcohol, allergies, celiac disease, gluten and wheat intolerance, parasites, diet, and autoimmune disease.

Autoimmune disease can cause leaky gut syndrome and vice versa. Once you have a leaky gut, or autoimmune disease, there are many foods that can trigger a flare-up. Vegetarian proteins are especially problematic for triggering an immune response, putting the vegetarian Empaths more at risk. Wheat and refined sugar are also high on the list for causing and triggering an attack. Here are some others: most grains, gluten, dairy, alcohol, eggs, nuts and seeds, legumes (including soya), alcohol, potatoes, eggplants, tomatoes, chilies, and processed foods.

The Signs

If you work to balance the mind, body and spirit, and have removed alcohol, wheat and sugar from your diet, yet still suffer with physical ailments, consider the possibility you may have autoimmune disorder. Some simple changes to the diet can help keep an autoimmune disorder at bay. Autoimmune can be diagnosed by a specialist or a good functional medicine practitioner. I will also list a couple of websites in the reference section where you can get free and helpful advice on the subject.

Everyone is here for a reason and each has a purpose to fulfil. If you are being poisoned by the food you eat you will never reach your true potential. The fear, anxiety, brain fog, intense fatigue, depression and emotional overload, certain drug-like foods cause, holds you back from whatever it is you are here to do. They also heighten all the Empath's negative traits and supress the more positive ones. By eating toxic, drug-like foods, you will not have the energy or inclination to take part in any kind of life-fulfilling role.

Drug-like foods not only affect your health and Empath traits, they also affect your chakras and hormones. Until you rebalance your chakras, and thus endocrine glands, you will not find equilibrium.

Chakras and Endocrine Glands

During my yoga and metaphysical studies, I also studied the chakras: where they are located, how they work, what unbalances and blocks them. Although I learnt much about their workings, much of what I read was not written taking modern diet into consideration. It is known that when the hormones are out of sync so will be the corresponding chakras. Nothing upsets the smooth running of the hormones than drug-like foods.

Most of the world's food supply is now either processed, genetically altered, or modified, and filled with chemicals. This has a huge negative impact on the hormones, which is governed by the endocrine system, and thus the chakras.

Chakras are energy centers located along the central energy canal of the spine, in correlation with the endocrine system. The word chakra means wheel or circle and can be translated into vortex or whirlpool.

Chakras are the vortices which control the pranic energy within the body, they are considered to be energetic glands that represent a physical endocrine gland.

Ancient yogis have known for thousands of years the connection between the chakras and endocrine glands (producers of hormones). They knew when the chakras are in balance so would be the endocrine system and vice versa. There are some who scoff at the concept of chakras. Because they cannot be seen with the physical eye, some believe they are fictional. They need visual proof before they will accept chakras as bearing any relevance on the health. They are the same people who would question the authenticity of an Empath's abilities. Empaths themselves, however, tend to be more open to the concept of energetic glands. Not only because they are more aware of the power of invisible energies but because they may sense the subtle energy of the chakras.

Chakras and Their Linking Glands

Root or base chakra: *adrenal glands*

Sacral chakra: *ovaries/testes*

Solar plexus chakra: *pancreas*

Heart chakra: *thymus gland*

Throat chakra: *thyroid/parathyroid glands*

Third eye chakra: *pineal gland*

Crown chakra: *pituitary gland*

Chakra Balancing

The endocrine system is a collection of glands, within the body, that secrete more than 20 different hormones into the bloodstream. These hormones are like chemical messengers. Each one has its own purpose, working independently, but also synergistically within the body.

You may not be familiar with the endocrine system but you will be familiar with some of the glands and the hormones they secrete: The pineal gland secretes melatonin and serotonin, the thyroid secretes thyroxin, adrenals produce adrenaline, the pancreas releases insulin and the testes and ovaries secrete estrogen and testosterone.

The endocrine glands react to specific stimuli and will release hormones for the body to carry out a certain function. For example: in darkness, the pineal gland will produce melatonin, the sleep hormone, which tells the body it is time to sleep. In times of fear, the adrenals ramp up production of adrenaline which gives you the strength to run away from a dangerous situation, and when you consume starchy carbohydrates, or sugars, your pancreas releases insulin which the body uses to remove excess sugar from your bloodstream to use for energy.

Your chemical messengers have their own functions, with the organs and tissues, but they also work together. When one goes out-of-balance it has a knock-on-effect on the others. Modern diets and lifestyles create a discord within the endocrine system.

Certain foods or stimulants encourage excessive production of particular hormones. Wheat or sugar, for example, cause an overproduction of insulin. Too much coffee (caffeine) will produce excess cortisol and adrenaline. These effects not only act as a catalyst for weight gain but also upset other glands. This happening every now and again is not a problem but for most people it is happening every day.

By consuming drug-like foods, which make you anxious, the body then produces more stress hormones such as cortisol and adrenaline. An overproduction of these hormones causes a fearful state.

When gripped by fear, your thoughts darken and you become more fearful or anxious. This then causes more cortisol production. Being tricked into believing there is a real danger, the endocrine glands responds by flooding the system with adrenaline to give a rush energy. This is glucose energy which is not needed. The body has been put on high alert for no reason

163

and has to produce insulin to clear out the unused to glucose. This repeatedly happening, will eventually lead to anything from weight gain to diabetes.

The Overstimulated Mind

It is not just the diet that puts the energy glands out-of-balance, stress and negative thought patterns are equally problematic.

Untamed, negative thoughts turn into painful emotions, these emotions travel to the parts of the body associated with certain fears and weaken that area. It is easy to understand how thoughts turn into emotions If you command your heart to beat faster it won't do it, but if you imagine being followed, by a ghostly figure, down a dark, lonely pathway, this could certainly speed up the heart-rate.

You can also unnecessarily aggravate your emotions by the thoughts you choose to indulge. If, for example, you continuously think about injustices done against you, it will stir up uncomfortable emotions within. A typical emotion rattled by holding court with provoking thoughts is anger. This anger is normally felt in the area around the stomach or heart. Experience this emotion often enough and it may lead to disorders of that area, the corresponding chakra and endocrine gland.

Chakras can be open, closed, blocked or imbalanced. Ideally, when healthy, they should open and close naturally and not be stuck or blocked. They are affected by personal trauma, anxiety and stress, and can be forced permanently open by the regular use of drugs, drug-like foods, medications, excessive alcohol, smoking, and unresolved emotional pain. If they remain open the more likelihood of imbalance and leaky aura.

The aura and the chakras are connected. If the chakras are unbalanced the aura becomes weakened and leaky. An Empath's energy centers are already vulnerable because they often acquire the negative energy from others. If they regularly drink alcohol, take drugs, or consume food that acts like drugs, it can force the chakras open. Open energy centers are bad news!

Depending on the Sensitivity of a person will depend on the speed of which disorders show up in their body. High reactive people, like Empaths, get sicker sooner than those who feel less and have a thicker skin. This is another reason why the Empaths have to be extra vigilant about keeping their physical and energetic body's balanced, and keep their chakras flexible.

165

Stored emotional wounds can be cleared from the chakras by practicing the powerful chakra clearing meditation in the tools section. But unless they also embrace a more suitable lifestyle unbalanced chakras will continue to be a theme for the Empath.

Most Sensitive folk already have an inkling of what they should remove from their diet. Unfortunately, when it comes to healing their own body and mind, the Empath doesn't always listen to their inner-Knowing.

You are at the helm of your own ships. No one can force you to make a change, nor will change happen without you first taking the required steps.

When you commit to making essential, and sometimes uncomfortable, changes your life transforms. If you want to see real magic happen within your life get rid of what holds you back!

Once you embark on this journey of self-healing through cleaning up your diet and re-balancing your mind, you will be astounded at how your life shifts gears. Your intuition and happiness increases and information presents itself as and when needed.

You have to work at making changes to free your mind, heal your body and engage your spirit. Great, amazing and valuable lessons are learnt from enduring difficult and challenging times. But you only find freedom from emotional and physical pain by bringing into balance your mind, body and spirit.

The take-home message of this Secret is if you want to see BIG changes in your life, change your diet! Now onto the final Secret.

Secret 7

Empowering the Empath

Within this Secret I discuss a somewhat complex subject. But it is a matter of great importance for all Empaths to understand if they want to live happily and healthily in the world. This information is key to gaining emotional freedom and for finding their true power!

Once you have read this Secret you will gain an understanding of why Empaths have such heightened emotions, why their intuition, and observational skills, are so highly attuned and from where it is they get their title. It will also help you understand why you suffer overwhelm and fatigue, why you have such sharp senses and the ability to feel other people's emotional pain.

When you have finished reading, you will have all the tools you need to get back in control of your life and find the joy you were meant for. Yes, this is exactly how you are supposed to be living: blissfully and abundantly.

Without trying to sound conceited, I would like to point out that the Empaths are supposed to play a significant role in life. They are meant to help raise the vibration of their surroundings. When in balance, and radiating positive energy, they do this effortlessly. And they do so without even being aware. Unfortunately, too many Empaths have been taken out of action. Most do not understand why this has happened or how to fix it. This is what I hope to make you aware of within this book, and especially this final Secret.

When you feel painful emotions, and think dark repetitive thoughts, you put this energy out into the world. The same can be said for when you are in a positive emotional space, your energy becomes delightfully uplifting and infectious.

I have already discussed emotional contagion and how you can project your moods onto others. When tired, and suffering with brain fog, the Empath may see this reflected in those nearby. Or if emotionally flat, it may be mirrored by a coldness in the moods of those who they come into contact with. Because of energetic feedback, all humans have the ability to affect others with their emotional tone, but in those who are Sensitive this ability is much more distinctive.

Parts of an Empath's brain, responsible for processing emotional responses such as empathy and intuition, are hyper-reactive. Because their brain sensors have been in a heightened state for most of their lives, they were overly affected by the negative stimuli they experienced in their past. For example: being berated by an angry parent, or teacher, getting singled out by the school bully, having a fear of not fitting in, experiencing a death of a loved one, spending too much time around negative people, or being repeatedly hurt, are just some types of encounters that contribute to an Empath's vulnerability, emotional overload and inability to handle negativity.

It is not just the Empaths who react to negative situations, all humans are hardwired into focusing more on the negative than the positive. The brain's negativity bias, a protective reaction which stems back to survival instincts from caveman days, is a reaction which focuses your attention more towards the unpleasant. By keeping you alert to potential threats, this negativity bias is supposed to protect you from any unsuspected predators such as lions, tigers and bears. However, in modern day, there is little chance of bumping into a bear when walking down the high street. Most negativity bias threats are illusions and built within the mind. But, this matters little to an Empath. Once their focus has been taken to a negative, it often stays there.

It would seem the part of the brain which activates negative emotions is amplified in the Empath. And the part responsible for generating joy is less active. Those who have difficulty experiencing satisfaction often turn to alcohol, drugs, sugar-forming foods or caffeine, for a pleasure hit. But, what most don't realize, these stimulants contribute to keeping the pleasure forming part of the brain inactive.

To better appreciate the way of an Empath, it helps to understand a part of the brain called the limbic system. There is no easy way to explain the complexities of the brain but, luckily, I am only covering the parts that relate to the emotions, intuition and empathy.

What is the Limbic System?

The limbic system is a complex set of structures that lie on both sides of the thalamus in the brain. It includes the hypothalamus, the hippocampus, the amygdala, and more. It appears to be responsible for emotions and has a lot to do with the formation of emotional memories.

Hypothalamus

The hypothalamus is one of the busiest parts of the brain and is mainly concerned with homeostasis. Homeostasis is the process of returning something to its set point. It works like a thermostat on a heating system. When a building gets to a certain temperature the thermostat will turn off the heating. When the house gets too cool it will turn the heating back on.

The hypothalamus regulates hunger, thirst, responses to pain, levels of pleasure, aggression and more. It also regulates the function of the autonomic nervous system (sympathetic and parasympathetic nervous systems) which regulates the pulse, blood pressure, breathing, and provocation to emotional responses. The other way the hypothalamus controls things is via the pituitary gland. Known as the master gland, the pituitary pumps hormones into the bloodstream, which has a direct impact on all bodily systems and is therefore an important part of the brain.

Hippocampus

The hippocampus comprises of two horns that curve back from the amygdala. It appears to be very important for creating long-term memories. If the hippocampus is damaged, a person cannot build new memories.

The Amygdala

The amygdala is a set of small almond-shaped clusters of nuclei, located deep within the brain's temporal lobe. The amygdala plays a major part in processing emotions. The more aggressive the emotion, the more responsive the amygdala becomes. When activated, it initiates the release of the fight-or-flight hormones (cortisol and adrenaline). It has been scientifically proven that the amygdala is overactive in those who are Sensitive. This is known as having a hot amygdala'.

Insular Cortex

Another area of the brain involved in the function of the limbic system is the insular cortex. The insular cortex is a hidden lobe that lies deep to the lateral surface of the brain and is responsible for self-awareness, empathy and social discipline.

The Empath Brain

The limbic system plays a significant role in the Empath's wellbeing. It is when the limbic system is out-of-balance, the Empath herself becomes unstable and normal social functioning is affected.

Although it is the limbic system in its entirety which is out-of-balance in many Empaths, I will focus on just two aspects: the amygdala and the insular cortex.

The Overstimulated Amygdala

The amygdala is not a thinking part of the brain, it is a reacting part, which activates when exposed to certain stimuli such as stress, fear and other strong emotions and causes an automatic response known as the fight-or-flight response.

Dr. Elaine Aron, a research psychologist and self-proclaimed Highly Sensitive Person, has done much scientific research on the amygdala. In her studies, she found the amygdala is overactive in Sensitive people when in circumstances that incite emotional responses.

Aron, who studied at the Jung institute and has a thriving psychotherapy practices, found, through a series of trials and research, that when Sensitives were shown pictures of human suffering the amygdala became extremely active. She found this activation also released an excess of cortisol and adrenaline into the body. These hormones then further enticed undesirable emotional reactions known as the fight-or-flight response.

The Sympathetic and Parasympathetic Nervous System (SNS & PNS)

The sympathetic nervous system (SNS) is responsible for the fight-or-flight response and stimulates nervous energy. The SNS is activated in times of fear, stress or danger. The parasympathetic nervous system (PNS) keeps the body and mind healthy, relaxed and in balance. It is activated through various relaxation practices such as yoga, massage or specific breathing techniques.

Within the out-of-balance Empath, it is the SNS which is dominant. When the SNS is constantly on "fight-or-flight" mode it interrupts the natural flow of hormones and harmfully impacts the immune system, emotions, brain and muscle functions.

The fight-or-flight response is a protective reaction. The process elevates hormones to provide energy to run away from danger or to stay and fight. But, because the Empath's dangers are mostly invisible threats (stemming from thoughts, emotions or the energy of others), these hormones do not get used. This leads to a semi-permanent activation of the SNS, meaning the body is constantly on high alert. The body should be in this state only from time to time. But, in the Empath, it can become a near permanent state. This means the body produces excessive amounts of cortisol. Signs you have too much cortisol are: excess fat, especially around the belly area, feeling anxious or down, stomach problems, frequent backaches or headaches, low immune system, fatigue and an inability to sleep.

The Organ That Never Forgets

Because the amygdala retains all the emotional memories one has ever experienced, these stored memories have the potential to become trauma triggers. In experiments on caged rats, it was found when they received painful shocks, at the same time as specific sounds, they showed a stress response. However, at a later date, the same sound played without the shock would trigger a similar stress response. Although no shock was given, the rat was expecting to experience pain when he heard that sound. This was due the amygdala's ability to link a certain sound with pain. It also reacts the same in people.

The amygdala is the most involved brain structure in emotional responses and for creating emotional memories. The hippocampus transforms short-term memory into long-term memory, and conveys emotional significance to stored memories. The amygdala and the hippocampus work together to create long-term memories of all the emotional events experienced. This dual activation is what gives emotionally based memories their individuality.

When emotions are aroused, the brain takes note and it stores as much detail as possible about an emotion-filled event, ready for quick recall. The emotionally charged memory can then be called upon at a second's notice, even after a long time has passed. With time, the amygdala learns the level of danger which should be linked to any particular trigger and in the Empath's case, the trigger becomes people. If you do not retrain and rebalance the amygdala, those triggers cause more damage to the body and mind.

The amygdala not only cultivates emotions such as fear, anxiety, envy and feelings of threat, but, over the years, stores all the memories of everything that activated one of these emotional responses.

Having a hyper-reactive limbic system, means the Empath experiences emotions more powerfully than most. Every time the Empath has felt excessively uncomfortable, or overly fearful, the memory was then stored within the amygdala. This can even be traced back to childhood. Any past event that ignited strong emotions was stored in the amygdala. If an Empath spent time around someone overly negative who emotionally scarred them, being in the vicinity of someone with similar energy in the future will activate the amygdala's memory. If any issue was significant enough to ignite a negative emotion it is stored in the amygdala's emotional memory.

These hidden memories trigger inner turmoil. A single person, who caused emotional upset in the past, can activate the amygdala (a reason Empaths find it so hard to forgive), and this is why people become trauma triggers for the Empath.

There is an old saying that we should *'forgive and forget'*. Forgiveness is one of the most powerful things humans can do for their growth and emotional freedom. Not so easy for the Empath because they don't simply forget.

Emotional pain is hardwired into their brain. If the Empath feels anguish when they think of a certain person, then it is near impossible to forgive them. Also, if unaware why certain people make them uncomfortable they find it difficult to be in their presence.

A hot amygdala is mostly responsible for the emotional overwhelm an Empath suffers. And until they take back control, the amygdala will continue to activate to real and imaginary threats for a lifetime.

The amygdala also processes feelings relating to criticism or negativity. If, for example, as a child you were chastised for your inabilities to perform, academically or on the sports field, which produced a sense of shame or inadequacy, this was instigated by the amygdala. The Sensitive child experiences chastisement worse than others and the future implications of which run far deeper. In adulthood, this is seen as an excessive sensitivity to criticism.

The Insular

The Empath's ability to sense and experience the emotional pain of others—often deemed as 'the Empath curse'—is linked to having a highly-receptive insula.

The insula, also known as the insular cortex, is responsible for managing self-awareness, empathy, intuition and social discipline. It is linked with social emotions such as: love and hate, shame and disgust, gratitude and resentment, self-confidence and embarrassment, trust and distrust, empathy and contempt, approval and disdain, pride and humiliation, truthfulness and deception, atonement and guilt. It also triggers a range of bodily sensations which link to certain emotions such as: sharp pain, burning pain, cool and warm temperatures, itching, muscle contraction, muscle burn, tickling, flushing, hunger and thirst.

In times of humiliation the skin may flush. When feeling guilt the muscles may contract. When envious, there could be a burning sensation in the stomach and when nervous, excessive thirst may be experienced. The organ also generates a sense of disgust with socially unacceptable conduct and, through pleasure and pain, motivates higher levels of behavior.

Mirror neurons, within the insula, enable humans to sense the feelings of others. By being able to share pain and joy empathetically, the organ converted people into social beings. In Empaths, however, this works a little too well enabling them to over-feel people's pain and emotions.

Although an Empath is capable of sensing great joy in people, because of their heightened mirror neurons, this gift is greatly dialed down by their capacity to overly sense negative emotions. An Empath's neurotransmitters work overtime to pick up on the turbulently vexed emotions of others, especially if they, themselves, are prone to melancholy or aggravated moods (like attracts like).

The Empath's ability to sense the truth and feel physical and emotional pain, in those around them, is believed to be due to having a highly receptive insula. As are their intuitive and empathic abilities.

Being highly intuitive, empathic and sensing the truth of the world are considered as Empath gifts. But sensing emotional pain, or negativity in others remains to be an Empath's bugbear. The above traits are influenced by the limbic system's interpretation of stimuli.

Collectively, the amygdala and insular cortex are responsible for activating the chemical messengers (hormones) of the body. A fact that any woman, who has experienced a monthly cycle, will attest to, fluctuating hormones have a massive impact on a person's mood. Because the Empath's amygdala and insula cortex are highly reactive, it often means their emotional-governing hormones are heightened and erratic. A rush of potent mood-controlling hormones manipulates how an Empath interprets emotions, both their own and others, which can lead to unnecessary mood swings, depression, sadness, anger and even fatigue.

The Overactive Amygdala

As already discussed, not only has the amygdala been linked with heightened emotions it is also responsible for Empath fatigue! It has been discovered by a Harley Street physician, Ashok Gupta, that an out-of-balance amygdala is the root cause behind fatigue and other chronic health conditions. Gupta, who specializes in treating fatigue, found through research and trials, that many health conditions are caused indirectly by an overactive amygdala, most notably chronic fatigue.

Gupta realized most of the research done on the amygdala in the past only focused on its threat to the mental state. More recent research, however, shows the amygdala is involved in activating endocrine and immune system responses, via the limbic system. This activation is supposed to be protective but actually causes damage. He believes the main causes of abnormalities in the amygdala are genetic, but some irregularities are caused by intense stress, bacteria or disease.

It is likely that an Empath was born with a highly receptive amygdala and insular cortex. Meaning they were born vulnerable to experiencing an excess of heightened emotions, both their own and others, and they are far more likely to experience chronic fatigue (AKA Empath fatigue).

Through his research, Ashok Gupta found a combination of factors changed the circuitry of the amygdala and the insula, making them continuously over-stimulate the body. In association with the insula, the amygdala learns to be hyper-reactive to any emotional responses within the body. This is an unconscious reaction. If the amygdala and insula are constantly over-stimulated, by emotional responses, the seeds for chronic fatigue, and other health-related-issues, are sewn.

Gupta also discovered that over time the hyper-arousal of the body, via the amygdala and insula, causes secondary illnesses such as allergies and chemical sensitivities, it also stresses the sympathetic nervous system (SNS).

If the brain and body are on constant high alert, from the SNS being stressed, the amygdala—in association with other brain structures—is prone to learning new responses to stimuli it would not normally be concerned with.

When the SNS is activated, digestive and detoxification systems are turned down, or switched off. This offers an explanation as to why many Empaths feel physically ill or run down after being constantly overwhelmed by emotional responses. The more an Empath experiences, emotionally, from having a hyper-active amygdala, the weaker their body becomes, and the more likely they will suffer with Empath fatigue and other ailments.

Here are some other maladies Gupta found to be associated with having an out-of-balance amygdala (and thus limbic system):

Muscular Fatigue & Joint Pain: It is common to experience pain in the joints of the body such as: the back, knees, hips or wrists. Muscles easily tire, making the body feel heavy and lethargic.

185

Adverse Reaction to Exercise: Because the muscles are already exhausted from being tensed up all day (being activated by the sympathetic system) they find it difficult to respond normally to exercise and exhaust rapidly. For this reason, Empaths should keep their workout short but intense; more on this shortly.

Digestive Problems: The digestive system has its own nervous system, sometimes called the second brain. It becomes stimulated by the brain via the SNS during stress, and this causes problems in the gut. It can tense the colon muscles and over-stimulate the gut. Leading to symptoms of IBS: constipation, diarrhea, etc.

Immune System Problems: The immune system is always ready to respond to a threat. If the view of the threat is overstated it can lead to an unnecessary immune response. This explains the unusual allergy and flu-like symptoms, sore throats, headaches, swollen glands or other irritating maladies many Empaths suffer.

Food Allergies/Sensitivities: The gut can become sensitized to everyday foods it perceives as toxic or a threat (as explained in last secret). Any foods containing lectins (mostly plant-based) become problematic. The immune system is in a sensitized state and will over-protect itself. The body may become intolerant to foods previously eaten without a reaction.

Exhaustion and Sleep Disturbances: Studies show the amygdala is partly responsible for keeping people awake at night due to excessive cortisol production. An Empath's mind is often bombarded with thoughts, making it difficult to get to or stay asleep. This is made worse by a highly reative amygdala. The hypothalamus regulates sleep rhythms, and it is this brain structure which responds to signals from the amygdala, to stay alert.

Sight Problems: The muscles which house the lens of the eye are affected the same way the rest of the body's muscles are by muscular fatigue. This can blur the vision when looking near-to-far and vice versa. Night vision may also be affected.

Alcohol Intolerance: Alcohol induces a stress response by stimulating hormone release via the hypothalamus. The amygdala is conditioned to respond to this and will create an increased sensitivity to alcohol.

Chemical Sensitivities: When the amygdala and insula are on high alert the body is prone to learning new sensitivities, and reacting to new threats of which it would not normally react.

187

Poor Detoxification: When the body is in sympathetic stress mode, from too much cortisol production, non-essential systems are switched off. This includes part of the body's healing and repair systems. If this reaction is extended, as it is in most Empath's cases, there may be a build-up of toxins in the body. By activating the parasympathetic system, through relaxation, yoga or meditation, it will help gradually detoxify the body.

Foggy Head and Inability to Concentrate: Because the Empath mind is often in a state of heightened stimulation it can become easily exhausted. This results in an insufficient blood supply to the brain. This reduction contributes to brain fog. The mind is also on edge due to the excited state of the amygdala and finds it difficult to focus.

Problems with Memory: The hippocampus has a dual role; it provides short term memory retrieval and acts as a control which moderates the release of stress hormones. The hippocampus becomes damaged from chronic stress and cannot sufficiently carry out these dual roles. This means the formation of new memories in the hippocampus is repressed, which causes problems with short term memory.

Vulnerability to Stress: The constant arousal of the amygdala means stress hormones become poorly controlled. The world is then seen as being more dangerous than it is which creates more stress.

Anxiety and Depression: Stress hormones are known to increase emotional instability and can cause symptoms of depression and anxiety. The amygdala is deliberately trying to make you feel anxious to warn of danger. This danger doesn't exist and is not life threatening but, because the body is stressed, the amygdala believes it does.

Panic Attacks: Being prone to panic attacks is known to be mediated by the amygdala. Prolonged worry or emotional distress can allow the amygdala to become over-reactive and triggered by any negative signal from the body.

Belly Fat: I used to believe Empaths had an excess of belly fat to protect them from other people's emotions. I now know it is partly caused by picking up stressful emotions from others. Trauma energy activates the sympathetic nervous system. The amygdala then perceiving this stress as danger, floods the body with adrenaline and cortisol to give the strength to run away,

189

which doesn't get used. Cortisol is known as the fat storing hormone because if it doesn't get used it gets turned to fat.

Retraining and Re-Balancing

Fortunately, the amygdala and insular cortex can be retrained so they are not constantly on high alert. This involves activating the parasympathetic nervous system (PNS), re-balancing the left and right hemispheres of the brain and balancing the hormones.

By retraining parts of the brain, responsible for heightened fears and emotions, the limbic system communicates with other parts of the brain to tone down their hyper-activity. In doing this it positively transforms the natural pleasure-forming centers of the brain. Happiness and passion towards life is then reawakened and Empath fatigue is significantly reduced.

Making simple changes and committing to less than half an hour's physical and mental exercise each day will see the Empath's life transform. Anyone can commit twenty to thirty minutes a day.

When you start any new routine it always seems an effort. But it is only effort until it becomes routine. If I can do it, anyone can! If you want to live the most fantastical life imaginable the following steps will help you achieve it. Don't wait start making the changes today!

There is nothing out of the ordinary about the following steps but done together they create extraordinary results. The answers to Empath healing need not be complicated. It involves making simple changes to the lifestyle. That said, being simple does not make them easy. They are like pieces of a jigsaw, the more you do, the more you get to see the bigger picture. They are listed in order of importance. Starting with what we learnt in the last Secret:

Seven Steps to Transformation

1. Avoid Stimulants and Drug-Like Food
2. Increase Water Consumption
3. Exercise
4. Sleep in Complete Darkness
5. Practice Mind Stilling and Brain Balancing Exercises
6. Stop Hiding From Self
7. Perform Five Minute Muscle Isolation Relaxation

Now you know the steps you are taking, I will explain each in turn:

1. Avoid Stimulants and Drug-Like Food

This program will not work effectively if you consume stimulants or drug-like foods. Drug-like foods not only create a dependence but play havoc with the Empath's body chemistry. They ramp up the negative side of your gift and tone down the more positive; making it difficult to function. Drug-like foods affect the opioid receptors in the brain and make them hyperactive. This results in an inability to experience pleasure, and a sense of being cut off from life. If you consume anything addictive, you will not want to give them up and may well get angry at the thought. But you do come around to the idea.

The process of taking back your power is done in small steps as is eliminating the brain's chemically unbalancing substances. You have chosen to read this book for a reason: to find balance. If you are serious about making changes to your diet, and to your Empath life, you may be interested in the book: 'The Eating Plan for Empaths & HSPs'. It is packed with information about how certain foods affect the Empath. It offers a step-by-step plan, including recipes, to help with the transition away from drug-like foods.

When removing drug-like foods it should be done with awareness, because anything drug-like creates withdrawal symptoms within the first week or two of elimination. Expecting anyone to give up everything at once is too much. It has to be done gradually. I used to include alcohol, sugar, wheat and caffeine in my diet. I eliminated them over a period of three years. I gave up wheat first, alcohol next, then foods containing white sugar and more recently caffeine. Oddly enough the drug I eliminated last has had the worst side-effects. Caffeine is one of the most over-used addictive drugs available which keeps people in a hyper-stressed state.

The withdrawal symptoms I experienced, from caffeine, got so bad it made me question my decision to quit. This is the one drug I would not recommend quitting cold-turkey, especially if you drink a lot of coffee. Caffeine keeps the body in a highly-stressed state by stimulating the release of adrenaline. You may be fooled into believing caffeine gives you energy, it actually does the opposite. It stresses the adrenals. This action then weakens and overworks an already delicate body chemistry. If you drink coffee and become jittery or anxious, shortly after, your system has become too clean for caffeine.

Caffeine keeps the body in a state of high alert, expectant of impending danger, and switches on the sympathetic nervous system. Because of their Sensitivity, the Empath already has an overworked SNS and the last thing they need is more stimulation.

When giving up anything drug-like allow yourself at least four weeks and trust you will get over the dependency. As I've said before, transformation is not an overnight process, you have to believe in the process and listen to your intuition.

See the Tools section for more advice on how to give up drug-like food and drink.

2. Increase Water

The body is comprised of 75% water (some body tissue has 95%), so it should come as no surprise that you need to drink lots of it to promote proper brain function, detoxify the body and stay healthy. Empaths need a lot of water to stay in balance. You should treat water as your primary holistic medicine.

Many are unaware just how dehydrated they are. An insufficient supply of water creates problems with the functioning of the body and mind. It affects your well-being and appearance, and accelerates the aging process. Being well-hydrated is essential to keep the body functioning optimally and energy preserved. You could not survive more than a few days without fluid and this should make it clear how important it is.

Because they are often on high-emotional-alert, Empaths need a lot of water, both inside and outside their bodies. Water helps flush out the toxins and helps clear the energy field.

Dehydration can lead to mental and physical disorders. An insufficient supply of water creates problems with all functions of the physical and energetic bodies. Breathing alone loses a quarter of the body's water on a daily basis. If as an Empath, you allow yourself to get dehydrated you are more prone to suffering anxiety and panic attacks.

A lack of water shows up in the body in many ways: externally as wrinkly or tissue-like skin, dry mouth, lips and eyes. Mild dehydration can cause headaches, dizziness, brain fog and fatigue. It may also lead to muscle weakness and lack of stamina. Ongoing dehydration causes constipation, problems with the functioning of the kidneys and liver, and muscle and joint damage.

Dehydration also produces emotional stress, something Empaths already have too much of. Drinking plenty of water whilst enduring any type of stress, significantly reduces its negative effect on the body and mind. Water also helps diffuse and dilute negative energy picked up from others. It keeps the physical body strong and acts as a buffer to unpleasant energy.

Drinking water also helps ward off depression and low moods. F. Batmanghelidj, M.D., author of '*Your Body's Many Cries for Water*', says in his book:

"*Pathology that is seen to be associated with social stresses— fear, anxiety, insecurity, persistent emotional and matrimonial problems—and the establishment of depression are the results of water deficiency to the point that the water requirement of brain tissue is affected.*" He writes: "*With dehydration, the level of energy generation in the brain is decreased. Many functions of the brain that depend on this type of energy become inefficient. We recognize this inadequacy of function and call it depression.*"

Everyone should drink **at least** ten glasses of pure water each day to replenish what the body loses through sweating and urination. The heavier you are, and the more you sweat, the more water you should drink. As a general rule, if you are thirsty you are already dehydrated.

In a bid to stay hydrated it is necessary to keep an eye on your mineral levels. When you consume high amounts of water, or sweat profusely, sodium and essential minerals are flushed from the body. When you increase water consumption you should also increase your salt intake.

All salts are not created equal, at least not those bought in the supermarkets. The only mineral rich salt suitable for safe human consumption is either unrefined rock or sea salt and they must be organic.

Organic, unrefined salt is crystalline in structure and can easily be absorbed by the body. This is because the blood has a crystalline structure. Unrefined salt is packed with essential minerals vital for good health. My favorite is Himalayan crystal rock salt, which has the full spectrum of 84 trace minerals and elements (regular table salt has only 4). You can safely add this to your food, or allow a small particle to dissolve on the tongue, before slowly drinking a pint of clean fresh water.

When you increase your water intake you quickly see an improvement in your physical and mental well-being. You also

197

find your natural thirst develops which ensures you stay adequately hydrated.

3. Exercise

Doing some form of exercise is essential for the Empath. Not only does exercise work the heart, burn fat and keeps you healthy, it also promotes serotonin production.

Serotonin is a very important hormone for the Empath. It lifts the moods, makes you feel good and is a precursor for the body to produce melatonin.

Exercise also keeps your body strong and flexible. For the Empath, it also helps us deal with their own emotions and those coming from others. It literally burns them off.

When it comes to exercise everyone is different. Some love physically demanding sports and some love to do gentle yoga. From my research, and self-trials, I have come to understand we need both.

High intensity exercise works the heart, burns off energy, produces human growth hormone and release feel good endorphins. Yoga, or stretching exercises, keeps the muscles strong, flexible and less injury prone, it helps re-balance the endocrine glands and energy centers, calms the mind and reduces cortisol production.

High Intensity Interval Training/Exercise (HIIT)

HIIT may sound scary but it is simply working the body to its utmost capacity for a short duration of time. Low to moderate intensity intervals are alternated with high intensity intervals. HIIT is one of the best ways to get the body to produce human growth hormone.

Human growth hormone (HGH) is secreted by the pituitary gland in the brain and is crucial for growth and repair of the body's cells, and for strengthening the immune system. All of which are essential for the Empath.

HGH rises in childhood, peaks in puberty and declines from the thirties onwards. It is known to be beneficial for autoimmune diseases, healing wounds and injuries, and for staying youthful.

High intensity interval exercise (HIIT) activates the super-fast muscle fibers. These fibers are the only muscle fibers to produce HGH. A study published in 'Sports Medicine' found that just ten minutes HIIT exercise is enough to secrete human growth hormone. HGH can turn back the body's internal clock, helping you slash fat, build muscle and increase energy levels.

HIIT can be applied to running or walking. For example: you could spend eight minutes on a treadmill and walk for one minute then run for the next. Or, on a stationary bike, pedal as fast as you can for 50 seconds then slow right down for a minute, until you catch your breath, repeat again until your short allotment of time is up. As long as you put maximum effort into the short burst of exercise you are on the right track.

There are many HIIT techniques that can be performed at home or the gym. It is doable for everyone. As long as you are in good health and are willing to build up your fitness levels you are an excellent candidate for HIIT.

If you are unfit, or have not exercised for a while, speak to your doctor or a qualified fitness instructor about the best ways to build up your body, ready for high intensity interval training.

Yoga/Mindful Stretches

Amongst other things, yoga works on balancing the endocrine system. As already discussed, the endocrine system is part of the body's chemical messenger service which secretes hormones

200

into the bloodstream as and when needed. Cortisol is produced by the adrenal cortex; like adrenaline, it is produced in response to stress.

Empath stress can trigger the same hormonal response as danger. Practicing yoga, or mindful stretches, significantly reduces Empath stress, which prevents or reverses the damaging effects of cortisol. Unlike other forms of exercise, yoga looks after far more than just the physical well-being, it keeps one in peak mental and spiritual balance too. Practicing yoga can sooth the body's energy, relax the nervous system and reorganize neural circuits.

4. Sleep in Darkness

This is essential for the release of melatonin and for all Empaths. Melatonin is known as the anti-aging, immune-system-boosting sleep hormone and is produced by the pineal gland (area of third eye) in darkness.

Melatonin is a naturally occurring hormone that regulates the sleep cycle. It is an antioxidant and anti-inflammatory and helps prevent and treat many illnesses including cancer. Those suffering insomnia and sleeping difficulties are thought to have a melatonin deficiency. Melatonin slows down the aging process, decreases cholesterol, lifts the moods and makes you feel good.

Sleeping in the dark allows the immune system to carry out essential repair work. The immune system does most of its work at night and is believed to be interlinked with production of melatonin. When melatonin levels are suppressed, illness occurs. As you age the body produces less melatonin. To ensure you produce as much as you can, sleep in the dark.

Every cell in your body reacts to light, and because of this a sleep-mask is not enough to block out excess night-light. For melatonin to be produced, while you sleep, your bedroom needs to be pitch black.

Because of the way their brain is wired, and the constant emotional stress they endure, Empaths are vulnerable to low moods and having a weakened immune system. You need to take every step you can to make sure you are producing adequate amounts of melatonin, and sleeping in complete darkness helps this happen.

Melatonin is known to increase human growth hormone (HGH) and helps protect the mitochondria. Mitochondria are the energy centers of cells that act like power factories. They convert food into the energy which drives every process in the body. Empaths need to conserve and protect all their energy sources and by protecting their mitochondria it helps stockpile physical energy.

There is now so much light pollution that sleeping in complete darkness is difficult to do. Because of the street lights, even with the curtains closed, bedrooms stay on the light side. Also, phones, alarm clocks and televisions add to excess night-light. This hinders the production of melatonin and leads to a less than restful night's sleep. Investing in a blackout blind, or curtains, is an excellent outlay for the Empath.

An Empath's body has to work hard to repair damage caused by excess emotions. If you are not getting enough melatonin you won't sleep properly and essential repairs cannot be carried out. Just by blacking out your bedroom it will improve your sleep, health, wellbeing and happiness.

5. Mind Stilling and Brain Balancing

Stilling the mind and balancing the brain are essential steps to stop the ravenous, and often incapacitating, thoughts many Empaths endure. If you do not control your thoughts you will struggle to re-balance the amygdala, insula and limbic system.

Negative thoughts trigger negative emotions and negative emotions trigger negative thoughts, both of which activate the SNS. Meditation is one of the most powerful tools an Empath can use to dilute their thoughts and gain mastery of their mind. A committed daily practice serves in many ways: It helps release serotonin, strengthens the mind, body and spirit, and builds a powerful shield against negative energies, it also opens the intuition like nothing else.

Meditation re-programs the brain into better coping with negativity and helps the Empath deal with other peoples' thoughts, energy and emotions. Because it makes the Empath more peaceful it helps them deal with any negativity they may encounter. Meditation is also the foundation for building any kind of spiritual development.

Most Empaths find meditation difficult to get into because of their creative and over-active mind. Perseverance is all that is needed. Thoughts are addictive and difficult to break free from but, once the mind is reset, through meditation, thoughts can be switched off at will.

The best way to meditate, for better mind control, is with an erect spine; sitting in a straight-backed chair or in a comfy cross-legged or kneeling position on the floor. Keeping the spine straight and upright allows energy to flow and the breath to be calm. Some say lying down is the best way to meditate, but it is too easy to fall asleep and the opportunity to quieten the mind, consciously, is lost. I have included a powerful meditation in the Tools section of this book, which also effectively balances the chakras.

Brain Balancing Breathing Techniques BBBT

Brain balancing breathing techniques are a powerful way to activate the invisible psychic centers of the body. Breath-work is conscious breathing that works to remove the energetic blockages in the body. The have many healing and balancing qualities.

Breathing is automatic. You don't have to think about it, breathing just happens. When you learn to control the breath, and direct it, during certain exercises, amazing things happen! The brain, endocrine glands and energy centers can rebalance and intuition builds. Practicing breathing techniques daily, combined with meditation, is life-altering. In the Tools section I have added two breathing exercises that can be safely practiced without a teacher. They are incredibly powerful and practicing them regularly will help balance the left and right hemispheres of the brain, and bring calm to one's life. If wanting to develop a stronger breath-work or pranayama program, it is advisable to get a good teacher. Because it is so powerful, if not done properly, stronger breath-work techniques can create problems in the energy centers.

6. Stop Hiding from Yourself

Many Empaths (me included) have spent a lot of time hiding from the world because of the way it makes them feel. It is either too loud, too fast, too overwhelming or too painful to be in.

The problem is when you hide from the world you may also end up hiding from yourselves and try to block out buried pain. When you hide from pain, or deny it, you cannot heal or release it. The pain is then stored. Anything stored within the physical or energetic body builds and attracts more of the same. When you face, and accept, what you feel you are liberated from it.

No matter how in balance they are, an Empath we will always feel other peoples' pain and negative emotions, but when they stop hiding from themselves, and accept their truth, their journey becomes easier.

Empaths maybe susceptible to the dark energy, and emotions, of others but when in balance, and in full acceptance of who they are, they can face them head-on. Also, when they experience their own trauma-triggered-emotional-memories facing the truth of them helps release their hold. Once their hidden angsts are confronted and accepted the Empath becomes empowered and free from any unnecessary pain they carried. Which has the extra bonus of preventing the limbic system, in the brain, from firing up unnecessary responsive warnings. It really is as simple as that.

A good way to release pain is to take your awareness to where you feel the discomfort, breathe into it and acknowledge all you are feeling. Talk to your pain by repeating an empowering mantra. Here's an example: 'Even though I feel this emotion as pain I accept it is just my interpretation. Thank you for the experience. I now release you with love and gratitude.'

To stop hiding from yourself it is as easy as accepting who you are and all you feel. When you experience unpleasant emotional energy from others, or your own irrational emotions arise, note how they feel then let them go. Keep reminding yourself how strong you are. You would not have taken on this role in life if you could not handle it.

The Gift

Being able to experience the world the way and Empath does is a gift, but for most it feels like a curse. You may not yet see it as a gift but one day you will, once balance is achieved.

Although an Empath becomes easily unbalanced, in the body and mind, they can heal themselves if they choose. No one else can do it for them. There may not be an over-night way to reclaim the brain and become re-balanced, but as an Empath you are stronger than you know and you can do anything you put your mind to. As I mentioned earlier in the book, you have already experienced masses of emotional pain, yet you still get up each morning to face another day. You are powerful and you need not hide anymore.

When your emotions are erratic the ability to see clearly is impaired. What you face, when unbalanced, is not a true reflection of yourself. Drugs or drug-like foods and drink put the body and mind out-of-sync. They ·amplify negative energy. Meaning any negative emotion you experience, will feel ten

208

times worse than they should. Removing food and drinks that act like drugs is the hardest challenge you will face. Not because giving them up is difficult but because you may not want to. Once out of your system you will see exactly how they affected your Empath body and mind and kept you in hiding from your true-self.

7. Muscle Isolation and Relaxation

An Empath's muscles are continuously stimulated through the stresses of modern life and by their sympathetic nervous system being "constantly on".

The Empath's muscles store a lot of negative emotions and energy and their active mind keeps the muscles on high alert. Even the TV programs watched of an evening, have the effect of firing up the mind. This stimulation then arouses the muscles which further tenses them.

Even now, whilst reading this, you will be holding tension somewhere in your body. If you take your awareness to your face you may notice your forehead, jaw or eyes are not relaxed. If you travel further into the body you may find your shoulders hunched or your wrists extended back; this all creates pressure in the muscles and joints. I could go through the entire body but it's safe to say you will hold tension somewhere.

When muscles—or a muscle—are constantly contracted and alert they fuel the sympathetic nervous system SNS (fight-or-flight). Not only is this depleting the body of vital energy, which those who have low energy can ill afford to lose, but it is prematurely aging, raises the blood pressure and lowers the immune system.

In training the muscles to soften, through relaxation, it switches on the parasympathetic nervous system PNS. This in turn slows the breathing, lowers the blood pressure, initiates deep relaxation and allows healing to occur.

In yoga, it is known the relaxation exercise, at the end of a class, is the most beneficial part of the practice. When you relax your body through muscle isolation it allows the body and mind to reset; this is essential to an Empath's well-being.

Please see Tools in the next section for instructions how to perform full-body muscle isolation and relaxation. Other ways to relax the body is by having any kind of body massage. Reflexology, or Indian head massage, is another excellent way to relax and switch on the parasympathetic nervous system.

Conclusion

So, there you have it! You should now have a greater understanding of why, as an Empath, you have such a challenging time. But you also know what you can do to transform your life and find true Empath balance and bliss! It is in your transformations that you get to harness you hidden power. It's up to you. No one can do it for you Be the change, see the change, reclaim your power and live the life you were born to live!

Tools for Transformation

The following pages include your tools for transformation and steps to find balance. Starting with some extremely effective breathing techniques, then moving through to a brilliant chakra balancing meditation, a fantastic muscle isolation exercise, easy ways to stop Empath overwhelm, tips to go wheat and sugar free and finishing with ways to deal with withdrawal:

Alternate Nostril Breathing

This technique is an excellent way to quieten the mind and find inner-bliss. It does this by activating the parasympathetic nervous system and by balancing the energy channels. Practicing it regularly will help stabilize the left and right hemispheres of the brain. This contributes to restoring poise to the limbic system and your masculine and feminine energy. It can be done as preparation for meditation or anytime one is feeling out of sorts. Many people find alternate nostril breathing a great way to aid sleep or to calm the nerves before a stressful event.

Please note: when you first start controlled breathing techniques it is common to feel dizzy. If this happens stop, take a break and build up gradually.

Technique: Sit (or stand) in a comfortable position. Using your right hand, place your thumb on your right nostril and close it, inhale through your left nostril, cover your left nostril with your ring finger, lift the thumb and exhale through the right nostril, this is immediately followed by an inhale through the right, close the right nostril with the thumb and exhale through the left nostril. This was one round. Start by practicing for one minute and build up gradually. Remember, it is on the exhale that you swap the nostrils you breathe through.

Buzzing Bee Breath

This technique is exactly as it would suggest. It involves making the sound of a buzzing bee whilst exhaling.

The practice invigorates the thyroid, balances the hormonal secretions, triggers serotonin release, improves functioning of nervous system, aids relaxation, is beneficial for breathing disorders, activates the pituitary gland, improves concentration and cures insomnia.

Technique: Sit in a relaxed position with the spine erect. Cover your ears by gently placing your thumbs over the opening. Place your index fingers on the forehead and let the remaining 3 fingers close your eyes. Inhale and take a slow deep breath, keep your mouth closed and begin slowly exhaling whilst making a bee-like humming sound, 'hmmmm'. Repeat three to five times and gradually build up the repetitions.

Mediation to Balance Chakras

This meditation is the most powerful one I have used for balancing the chakras and bringing calm.

It has an immediate effect and is excellent for grounding, uplifting and energizing. The technique came to me whilst in meditation. It can be done in five minutes or twenty-five, depending on your time availability.

Before you start make sure you will not be disturbed. Maybe light a candle or some incense.

- Sit in a comfortable position with your back straight and eyes closed.

- Quieten the mind by doing a few rounds of alternate nostril breathing.

- Take your awareness to your third eye (center of forehead). See a beautiful silver light building within your head. This is your own divine light.

- Take the silver light down through your body and see it connecting with your base chakra (base of spine). From here see the cord of light spiraling down, going deep into the center of the earth, grounding you firmly.

- Keeping the connection, follow the spiraling silver light back up through the earth, through the base chakra and upwards through your body, back up to the third eye.

From here take the silver light through your crown chakra and see it spiraling way up into the sky, all the way up till it connects with the Sun. Allow the powerful force of the Sun to charge the silver cord of light.

- Keeping the connection, follow the silver light back down through the crown chakra and back into the body. Feel the healing power of the Sun, our divine life-force, fill the body from the head to the feet. This is a celestial connection between the Sun and the Earth. (If in a hurry, the meditation can be finished here, but include the last step of the meditation.)

- Now take your awareness to your root chakra situated near the pelvic floor. See it spinning, red and vibrant, a distance of 15cm from the front of your body and going through to 15cm past the back of your body. Use the sliver sun-charged light to cleanse any emotional debris from your spinning energy center, going from front to back. Silently repeat: I restore you to balance. When you feel the base chakra is cleared move up to the next.

- Take your awareness to the orange sacral chakra spinning below the naval. See it at a distance of 15cm from the front of your body and going through 15cm to the back. Use the sliver sun-charged light to cleanse any emotional debris from your spinning energy center, front to back. Silently repeat: I restore you to balance. When you feel it is cleared move up to the next.

- See your yellow solar plexus chakra, located mid-stomach, spinning 15cm from the front of your body and going through to the back. Use the sliver, sun-charged light to cleanse any emotional debris from your spinning energy center, front to back. Silently repeat: I restore you to balance. When you feel it is cleared move up to the next.

- See your green heart chakra spinning in front of your heart, 15cm from your body and going through to the back. Use the sliver light to cleanse any emotional debris from your spinning energy center. Silently repeat: I restore you to balance. When you feel it is cleared move up to the next.

- See your blue throat chakra spinning at the front of your throat and going through to the back. Use the sliver light to cleanse any emotional debris from your spinning energy center. Silently repeat: I restore you to balance. When you feel it is cleared move up to the next.

- See your indigo third eye chakra spinning at the front of your forehead and going all the way through to the back.

  Use the sliver light to cleanse any emotional debris from your spinning energy center, front to back. Silently repeat: I restore you to balance. When you feel it is cleared move up to the next.

- See your violet crown chakra spinning at the top of your head, front to back. Use the sliver light to cleanse any emotional debris from your spinning energy center. Silently repeat: I restore you to balance. When you feel ready allow the silver-sun-charged light to expand around your body.

- Allow the powerful silver light to surround you in a beautiful halo. Engulfing you in protective healing energy. Know this light is your invisible shield of armor protecting you from any harm or negativity. Stay as long as you want in this relaxed state. (This step also finishes the shorter version of the meditation)

- When ready, gently open your eyes and take some deep refreshing breaths. Well done! You're good to go.

Muscle Isolation Relaxation Exercise

This technique can be practiced any time of the day but is excellent to do every evening before sleep. It aids in turning on the parasympathetic nervous system; which promotes sleep and allows for healing and maintenance work to be carried out during sleep.

To relax the body it needs to be in a supine position, lying on the floor or a bed, with the whole body weight supported (for anyone suffering back problems: a bolster or cushion under the knees is helpful).

The best way to relax a muscle is to tense it first, for five to ten seconds.

- Start at the feet and work up through limbs, torso and face, tensing each body part in turn for a count of up to ten seconds. When you have done this, go back through the body and allow each body part to relax.

- Take your awareness to your feet and say silently in your head: My feet are relaxed. Feel all tension melting out of your feet.

- Next move to you lower legs and say silently to yourself: My lower legs are relaxed. Feel any tension melting away.

- Repeat this technique all the way up the body, through your upper legs, buttocks, stomach, chest, back, neck, arms and hands repeating the same mantra, until you come to your head. Then repeat silently: My face and head are relaxed. Feel your head become like a lead weight. See there is no tension held in any part of your face. Swallow once and take a deep calming breath. Feel yourself drift off into a relaxing slumber.

Not only does this exercise promote relaxation but it will also assist in stilling the mind. It is great to do as an aid to sleeping (better than counting sheep). If time is short, or if you are feeling particularly sleepy, instead of doing each limb individually you could do the lower part of body first, then upper half and finish on the head and face.

Full muscle relaxation can be done anytime but try to perform it every evening before sleep. It is also great to do after exercise when the muscles have been stretched and strengthened and the mind is quieter.

5 Ways to Stop Emotional Overload.

The overwhelm an Empath feels when they've taken on too much emotional energy can be unbearable.

Emotional overload affects every Empath differently; some much worse than others. It can cause distress and misery, and triggers thoughts that keep you awake at night and darken your moods for days.

The following are some excellent quick-fix ways to stop the overwhelm in its tracks!

1. **Eat a small amount of chocolate**: I say small amount because large amounts have the opposite effect (I discovered this the delicious way, by devouring too much). Chocolate can transform and uplift your mood in an instant.

    Containing compounds which promote happiness, chocolate is the go-to food when you have been emotionally or energetically overwhelmed.

    Serotonin is a neurotransmitter, produced by eating chocolate, known as the happy hormone. As well as activating your bliss centers, it also stops you dipping into dark thoughts.

In my opinion, milk chocolate works better than dark, as the dark stuff contains a higher amount of caffeine. But this is something you can experiment with. Most chocolate contains refined sugar, which is a big cause of depression, not just in Empaths but all humans, so keep chocolate only for when you've been hit by an emotional overload.

Eat between 2 to 4 small squares of chocolate washed down with a pint of cool water. The water speeds the process up.

2. **Temple hold**: Place two to three fingers on either side of the temples (between the eyebrows and hairline) and hold for as long as needed.

This simple technique helps break the repetitive thoughts that are triggered from emotional pain. It also blocks the dense feelings they cause.

I'm not sure why this method works but it does. (I suspect it is because it activates the acupressure points

223

and soothes parts of the brain responsible for emotions.) It is great to do at bedtime when emotional overwhelm turns into rampant thoughts that keep you awake. Taking some calming, conscious breaths at the same time further helps.

3. **Short bursts of high intensity exercise**: A mini power walk or run, dynamic yoga moves, dance routines or skipping, etc. burns off raging emotions. I'm talking very doable bursts of exercise that last between 1 to 5 minutes.

Performing short bursts of high intensity exercise releases endorphins into the body which block the pain transmission signals and produce euphoric feelings that calm the entire system.

A great exercise I do, when I have been emotionally fired-up, is the plank. Most will have heard of the plank; it is a challenging yoga move that activates all the muscles in the body. Maintaining it for just 30 seconds is often all it takes to blast out the negative emotions that cause overwhelm.

There is a variation of the plank to do whatever your fitness level, from beginners and beyond. You will find plenty of excellent instructional videos on YouTube to get you started.

Whatever exercise you choose, as your mini blast, make sure to do something that makes you feel uncomfortable and your muscles burn. (The saying 'fight fire with fire' springs to mind here).

4. **Singing**: This is not always something you want to do when feeling low, but singing lifts your moods and is certainly worth trying when feeling overwhelmed.

    Singing raises your vibration and stops emotional overwhelm in its tracks. Anyone can sing, hum or chant. Just make sure it is an uplifting song and not one that stokes up painful emotional memories. Try it and see.

5. **Avoid caffeine**: Being a stimulant, caffeine will heighten any emotional overwhelm you are experiencing.

    You don't always realize that it worsens the emotions you feel, because caffeine only kicks in 30 to 40 minutes after consumption. It can make you anxious and jittery and anything you feel negatively inside is amplified. Not having caffeine will not stop emotional overload but it significantly reduces the symptoms, and that is why it is on the list.

Tips to Keep Wheat and Sugar Out of Your Life for Good

Be Prepared: When out and about, going to friends, work or anywhere take snacks in case you get hungry. Nuts are brilliant for this as they are both balanced and filling.

Bake and Freeze: When baking wheat-free breads or pizza bases, always make more than needed so you can freeze for a later date.

Make Wheat-Free Breadcrumbs: When cooking from scratch, wheat-free bread crumbs are handy to have in the freezer for making fish cakes, sausages or burgers. Pop stale wheat-free bread into a food processor and blitz till bread becomes crumbs. Freeze in batches.

Always Read Labels: Wheat and sugar are hidden in many foods, it is essential to check the labels.

Don't Be Fooled into Thinking a Little Won't Hurt: It only takes a tiny amount of wheat or refined sugar to reignite the addiction and it only takes a tiny amount of wheat to create a negative bodily reaction. A slither of cake here or a biscuit there may seem harmless but it will put you on a fast-tracked-path back to being a wheat and sugar addict.

Keep Your Diet Varied: Feeling bored or restricted by your diet can lead to being tempted to snack on a sugary or wheat treat. Keeping your diet varied will help you avoid temptation. Stay inspired by trying out new recipes for meals and snacks.

Always Phone Ahead When Eating Out: There is nothing worse than getting to a restaurant to discover the only thing you can eat is fries and a side salad. Numerous eating establishments now cater for special dietary requirements, but it is advisable to phone ahead first. Many eateries will allow you to bring along your own bread, pasta or pizza bases if they do not offer a wheat/gluten-free option.

Keep Your Cupboards Well Stocked: Always keep in a good stock of wheat-free cooking ingredients: fresh fruit and veg, eggs, seeds, ground almonds, wheat-free flours, unrefined sugar, honey or maple syrup, pulses, herbs and spices, rice,

227

wheat-free pasta etc., so you can easily whip up snacks, treats or meals.

Use Honey, Molasses, Maple Syrup or Unrefined Sugar in Cooking: These natural sweeteners not only add a delicious sweetness to your dishes but also have nutritional value.

Keep Stevia Sweeteners with You at all Times: If you are one who likes to have sweetness in your beverages, stevia or xylitol is a good replacement and a much healthier option than having aspartame sweeteners.

Giving Up Alcohol

If you have severe alcohol dependence it is a good idea to seek professional help before quitting. But if you consider yourself to be a social drinker, stopping is as simple as making the decision to quit.

For the first three or four weeks it is a good idea to avoid any social events that may tempt you into drinking alcohol. It is advisable to tell no one of your intentions; doing so just puts pressure on you. Find replacement drinks that do not include refined sugar. Sparkling water with freshly squeezed lime or lemon is a perfect.

Visit www.hellosundaymorning.org for tips and advice on how to quit alcohol for good.

Keep your intentions and resolve. You can do anything you put your mind to. That is the power of an Empath. If you want to see a transformation happen in your life, it is a small sacrifice.

Addictions and Withdrawal

Anything that creates an addiction normally has a withdrawal period. Withdrawal can last from a few days to a few weeks. You can get withdrawal symptoms from wheat, sugar, alcohol and caffeine. Following is a list of symptoms you may experience:

Emotional Withdrawal Symptoms

- Anxiety or panic attacks
- Restlessness
- Irritability
- Insomnia
- Headaches
- Poor concentration
- Depression

- Social isolation

Physical Withdrawal Symptoms

- Sweating
- Racing heart
- Palpitations
- Muscle tension
- Tightness in the chest
- Constipation
- Tremors
- Nausea
- Flu-like symptoms

Ways to Heal and Deal with Withdrawal

Hydrate: Drinking lots of water helps the body detoxify and flush out impurities caused from withdrawal.

Salt: When drinking lots of water essential minerals get flushed from the body. It is important to replace minerals with a good trace element salt such as Himalayan Rock Salt. Add small amounts to food or allow a particle to dissolve on the tongue.

Magnesium: Taking magnesium supplements helps relax muscles. It also helps bowel movements for those suffering constipation.

Rest: Sleep as much as your body needs. The body goes into shock when drugs are removed and will need more sleep and rest than normal.

Aromatherapy Baths: Taking a relaxing bath, with a few drops of lavender, is a perfect way to unwind and de-stress when in withdrawal. The essential oil works with the limbic system to help the body and mind relax and find equilibrium.

Other Books by Diane Kathrine

The Eating Plan for Empaths & HSPs - *The Easy Permanent Path to Emotional Freedom, Weight-Loss, Health & Happiness*

Empath Power *– Grounding Healing and Protection for Life!*

Traits of an Empath Uncovered *– Discover Who You are & Why Your Here*

The Empath Awakening *– Navigating Life in the Sensitive Lane*

Diane blogs at: www.theknowing1.wordpress.com

7 Secrets of the Sensitive

References for Secret 7

and

Further Reading

Empaths Empowered. My blog with lots of helpful information on grounding, healing and life as an Empath: www.theknowing1.wordpress.com

Dr. Elaine Aron's website and blog detailing research on the brain of Highly Sensitive People: www.hsperson.com

Free and Helpful Websites for Autoimmune Sufferers: www.autoimmunewellness.com, www.thepaleomom.com

Dr. Gupta's website research on chronic fatigue, amygdala and the insula: www.guptaprogramme.com/causes-of-me/

Explanation how mirror neurons work in the brain:

www.effective-mind-control.com/mirror-neurons.html

Information on the insular cortex and amygdala:

www.effective-mind-control.com/insular-cortex.html

Easy breakdown of the limbic system:

http://webspace.ship.edu/cgboer/limbicsystem.html

Information on the limbic system:
https://www.dartmouth.edu/~rswenson/NeuroSci/chapter_9.html

Research on empathy and physical sensations:
http://www.nytimes.com/2007/02/06/health/psychology/06brain.html?_r=2

7 *Secrets of the Sensitive*

Made in United States
North Haven, CT
16 November 2021